CALM IN THE STORM:

How God can Redeem a Crisis to Advance His Kingdom

Dr. Rob Reimer

Calm in the Storm: How God can Redeem a Crisis to Advance His Kingdom

Cover Design by Darcy Reimer

Printed in the United States of America

ISBN: 9798646638534

Table of Contents

Acknowledgements:

I want to thank the people who helped make this book a reality. First, I want to thank my family. This was a team effort with two of my kids, Danielle and Darcy, joining in the production. Danielle was instrumental figuring out how to publish on Amazon, a new experience for me, and I couldn't have done it without her. Darcy did the cover design – it is now the second book she has designed with me and she is a very talented young lady (She can be reached at DarcyReimerDesign@gmail.com). You've been great – thanks for helping out! Jen helped out in productions and marketing. You are a worthy partner in life and business! Grateful for all your help guys!

I also want to thank Tricia Peters for helping with the editing process. She volunteered and made it a better book in the process. Thank you for lending me your expertise.

Lastly, I want to thank God who redeems all things. I have been through many crises in the past, both personally and in life and ministry, and You have redeemed them all! Forever grateful!

Dedication:

This book is for my four children: Danielle, Courtney, Darcy and Craig. You will never know until you have children of you own how much you are truly loved. Such is the nature of parenting. When I held each of you in my arms for the first time, I felt like the Grinch on the old Christmas classic cartoon, whose heart grew three sizes larger. I had no idea of the human heart's capacity to love until you came into my life.

Sometimes I ask people, "If you could do life over, what would you do differently?" I am amazed at how many people respond, "I wouldn't change a thing." Not me. I don't think anyone can live life with sincere humility and authentic love and not experience regret. I don't carry my regret as a curtain of shame in my inner being thanks to Jesus, but if I could start life over, I would do a lot of things differently. Most of the things I would do differently come down to being a better husband and being a better father. I would be more attentive and less pre-occupied. I would be more patient and less hurried. I would capture more moments, create more memories, ask more questions, listen more carefully, love more tenderly and engage more fully.

There are two things I want you to know above all else. First, you are deeply loved by God and by your mother and me. There is nothing you could do that would make me love you less. I remember when you were little, I was baffled by the fact that after I gave you a time out you would not come over to me for a hug. I wanted to communicate to you that even if you did something wrong, you were still loved. I asked a child psychologist who was a friend about your avoidance, and she said it was the universal response of children after they have been corrected, even gently. She said, "They don't believe they can be naughty and still be loved." That was shocking to me, so I decided to put it to the test. I went home and called Danielle over to me and asked, "Does Daddy still love you when you're naughty?" She shook her head emphatically and said, "NO!" like that was the most ridiculous thing she had ever heard. As the rest of you got older, I asked you the same thing and you all gave the same response. So, I told each of you, "Of course I love you, even when you're naughty. Do you know why?" You didn't. I assured you that it was because God made you just for me. And that has never changed. You are deeply loved, not because of what you do, but because of who you are. You are my children.

The second thing I want you to know is that God is good and God is trustworthy. I think the secret to success is to find what God wants and do it. Life works better when we are in alignment with God. He is truly good. The world is broken, marked by evil, and stained by sin. All of that has distorted our view of the goodness of God, but the ultimate proof that God is good is the cross. Jesus became one of us. He entered into our pain. He took up our brokenness. He got marked by evil oppressors who falsely accused Him, unfairly tried Him, and unjustly nailed Him to a cross. And He was stained by sin, which he cleansed by His blood. I may not always understand everything that happens in this evil-infested planet, but I know God is good because of the cross. I know He wants our best. I have learned to trust Him; it hasn't always been easy, but I always come back to Jesus and the cross. Life is hard, but God is good. I have had to learn to separate out life from God. Life is life, and life is difficult. God is God, and God is good.

When I took you off to school for the first time I came home and sobbed. Mom cried with me for a bit and then she went into the other room. When she came back much later, I was still sobbing. She said, "What is wrong with you?" She wasn't being mean; she just didn't understand. I knew you were no longer under my protection and care, but I was releasing you into a world filled with sin and suffering. I was crying for all of the grief and pain that you would experience in this cruel world. I knew that your innocence would be lost, your hearts would be broken, people would be cruel, you would get hurt, and your dreams would get dashed over the course of your lifetime. And that day I grieved for all of the hurt this world would hand you. I have cried many secret tears for your pain ever since, and I have coupled those tears with the vigilant prayer that God would redeem all of the pain in your life. Only God can touch evil and make good from it, and that has been my prayer for you.

There are many things in life I would not have chosen, but I would not be the person I am today without passing through those dark corridors.

I would have protected you from these same difficulties, if I could, but these hardships are often the very things that strengthen us and shape us to become the people we have potential to become. This book is about how God redeems hardships and crises to shape us. I've been praying that over your life since God brought you into my life and I will continue to pray it over you until I breathe my last breath.

I am glad God gave you all to me. You are good people and I am proud of you. You have caring hearts and are marked with kindness. You have made my life better. I have laughed harder, cried longer, felt deeper and loved fuller because of you. I have loved being your father. I have loved having you in the house. I love the sounds of your laughter. I love the way you get along with each other. I delight in having you as my family. I am glad we are together. I will hate to see you go when the time comes.

If I could line up all of the children in the world, and I could only choose four, do you know who I'd choose? Danielle, Courtney, Darcy and Craig. Every time! Thanks for being mine. I love you, Dad.

Calm in the Storm: How God can redeem crisis and advance his Kingdom

Jen and I were on a plane ride from Newark to Cozumel. We were looking forward to getting away for a few days. We were both quietly reading a book when we heard a frantic flight attendant screaming, "There's a fire in the cockpit! There's a fire in the cockpit!" Not the kind of thing that sets you at ease when you are 30,000 feet up in the air. The mood on the planet noticeably shifted as voices rose in disbelief. Then she came running back down the aisle yelling, "Brace! Brace! Brace!" Some people started screaming; other people were crying. One lady in front of me fainted and her husband was slapping her in the face trying to wake her up – which even in the panic was funny to watch. I leaned over to Jen, kissed her gently on the cheek and said, "If we die, it's been a good life and I love you." Then I went back to reading my book. The flight made an emergency landing in Tampa Bay. There were fire trucks and emergency vehicles all over the runway as we made our landing. As we landed, I checked my pulse and it was 60. They took the flight attendants off the plane on gurneys.

My calm was as real and sure as my home in heaven. Secure eternal roots help us to navigate a current crisis with a calm interior.

My brother, Ken, tends to get choked up in key sentimental moments. We had a surprise 25th anniversary party for my parents when we were in our early twenties and my brother stood up to give the speech. He broke down and couldn't speak. I stood up, put my arm around him and said, "This is where I rescue him." Everyone laughed. He composed himself and was able to finish his speech. He was the best man at my wedding and when he stood up to give the speech, he broke down again and couldn't speak. I stood up, put my arm around him and said, "This is where I rescue him." Of course, many people who were at my parents 25th were also at my wedding and they roared with laughter. I was my brother's best man a year later and gave the best man speech without any need of rescuing. And a man who had been at all three events came up to me afterwards and said to me, "You are the ice man!" Not really. I've been rattled many times in my life. Peace isn't always easy to come by, especially in life's darkest moments, but it is available to us in Christ. And if we can learn how to access this supernatural peace, this crisis can become an opportunity to advance the Kingdom of God.

Jesus is never nervous

Jesus was deeply composed; He was never rattled. He was a man of peace. I think about the story of Jesus calming the storm. What strikes me isn't just that Jesus had the ability to calm the storm, but that Jesus Himself was calm in the storm. Asleep actually. Sound asleep – in a storm that terrified professional fishermen. The disciples woke Him in utter terror and said, "Teacher, don't you care if we drown?" Sheer panic had penetrated their souls. Yet, neither their panic, nor the convulsing storm rattled Jesus, not even a little. Mark 4:39 says, "He got up, rebuked the wind and said to the waves, 'Quiet! Be still!' Then the wind died down and it was completely calm. He said to his disciples, 'Why are you so afraid? Do you still have no faith?'" Wow!

Lots of people preach this passage and say things like, "Jesus will calm the storms of your life." Actually, I don't believe that, and I don't think we can use this passage to preach that either. Listen: Jesus may calm a storm in our life, but there are plenty of times He allows them to disrupt the landscape of our lives and He doesn't rescue us at all. There are plenty of passages that tell us we will have troubles in this life, even persecution; In John 16:33 Jesus said, "In this world you will have trouble. But take heart! I have overcome the world." Jesus never promised to protect us from all of the hardships or difficulties of life. I am not interested in Jesus calming our storms, or taking away our problems, but Jesus' calm in the storm and how that can be made available to us. How is it that Jesus was so calm in a storm so terrible that hardened fishermen were scared to death? How is it that Jesus expected them not to be afraid, but to have faith even in terrifying circumstances? How do we develop the interior life that allows us to stay calm when our exterior world is falling apart? How can we become the kind of people who can capitalize off of crisis to advance the Kingdom of God?

Current Crisis: COVID-19

How can we access the calm of Jesus in the chaos of life? As I write this, we are currently undergoing the most unique crisis of my lifetime: COVID-19, the Coronavirus. In all of my 55 years, I have never seen anything like it. I live right outside of New York City; it is a ghost town right now. People are panicked. All gatherings over ten people are forbidden. All non-essential businesses have been closed. People are told to stay in their houses. Everyone has to practice social distancing – keeping six feet apart. Grocery stores are often emptied of basic supplies – meat, pasta, bread – and toilet paper! Sheer panic. But if Jesus were with us in this boat, He would be calm in the storm. Jesus isn't nervous – not now, not ever. He hasn't been nervous in the past two thousand years as the world has suffered plagues, and famines, world wars and Great Depressions and He isn't nervous in heaven over this moment in time either. That is one of my favorite things about Jesus. The disciples turned to Jesus in their panic precisely because He was calm in the midst of the storm; Jesus is calm in the midst of every storm. We must develop the inner life that can allow us to become an anchor in the storms of our outer life. How do we become people like that for our times?

I have to believe things are going to get worse before they get better, but don't worry. I am not telling you this to make you fearful, quite to the contrary, I think we stand on the precipice of a unique historic opportunity. I'll come to that again in a moment, but first let's explore the potential problems that lie before us.

I think we may be headed toward the worst worldwide economic crisis that any of us who are living have seen. I'm not prophesying. I'm just observing; I have been saying this since they started shutting down businesses, but it is now beginning to be realized. My grandfather was a small businessman. He often had people work for him. If he was forced to shut down his business for months he wouldn't have survived. It would have forced him out of business and when the months passed, he would not have been able to re-open shop. All of the people who worked for him would have lost their jobs. He often lived month to month – the jobs would get done, he would get paid and he would pay those who worked for him and pay the bills in the house. But he couldn't survive without working. I think this crisis is going to force many small businesspeople out of business. The government aid will help some, for sure, but it won't solve all of the problems. I already know several local businesses that have been around for decades that have gone bankrupt in this season and have had to close their doors. The treasury department in the U.S. said this week that they expect unemployment to reach 20%. In the US over 33 million people have already filed for unemployment in the first seven weeks of the crisis, by far the most ever in our country's history. That's almost 20% of the adult population already and we aren't done yet.

Many large corporations will survive, but they will be forced to lay off many people if this crisis continues. It's just the nature of business. On April 15, 2020, the NY Times said that retail sales in the US showed their steepest drop on record; retail stores, they said, are now in a race to survive (New York Times, April 15, 2020, "'Pretty Catastrophic' Month for Retailers, and Now a Race to Survive"). If the isolation strategy continues, we may face the highest unemployment rate worldwide that we have ever seen. I'm not saying we can't recover, because I think we can. I am saying that I think there will be a very significant fallout from all of this mandatory staying home and the recovery will be slow and come at a great price. How long can we sustain not working and not expect some sort of dramatic economic implications?

There will also be an increase in domestic violence. You leave people home together in a high stress environment, and with no jobs, and alcohol still readily available and there will be an increase in domestic violence. Guaranteed. In New York City they have started advertising for domestic violence help at times when they give COVID-19 updates; they understand the reality of forced isolation.

I also read an article in the BBC which quoted Mark Woolhouse, a professor of infectious disease epidemiology at the University of Edinburgh, who said that this current strategy of social distancing that we are employing cannot work. He said that when we go back to work and back to life as normal, the virus will spread again; we will be faced with a fresh wave of outbreaks. He said that no country has an exit strategy – we don't have a plan to get back to normal. He said there are only three ways out: vaccination (which is 12-18 months away), enough people get the disease and develop immunities to stop the spread of outbreaks (which he says means at least 60% of people have the disease), or a permanent change of our behavior – or at least social distancing until we get everyone vaccinated. (BBC, March 20, 2020. James Gallagher, "Coronavirus: When will the outbreak end and life get back to normal?")

If we wait this crisis out and then send people back to work only to have another outbreak, then what? How bad will the panic be? How long can we stay out of work and not have a cataclysmic economic collapse? There are so many questions, so many unknowns, so many differing opinions and it is producing so much fear and angst. But Jesus isn't nervous. This is creating a potentially unparalleled opportunity for the church – but only if we are ready to seize it. In this book, I am not just concerned with helping believers to feel peace in this stormy season of life, I am concerned with the church preparing herself to be ready to seize an unprecedented kingdom opportunity.

Seek First His Kingdom

In the Sermon on the Mount, Jesus said, “Therefore I tell you, do not worry about your life, what you will eat or drink; or about your body, what you will wear. Is not life more important than food, and the body more important than clothes? Look at the birds of the air; they do not sow or reap or store away in barns, and yet your heavenly Father feeds them. Are you not much more valuable than they?” (Matthew 6:25-26). I was sitting with my cat yesterday and thinking about this passage in the midst of our current crisis and I have to say, my cat did not appear phased by all of this Coronavirus fallout; not even a little. He was completely unworried, marked by the total calm of the confidence that he would be cared for, his needs would be met, his next meal was not in jeopardy. He was peacefully at rest in the hands of a good master. Jesus finishes this passage with these words, “So do not worry, saying, ‘What shall we eat?’ or ‘What shall we drink?’ or ‘What shall we wear?’ For the pagans run after all these things, and your heavenly Father knows that you need them. But seek first his kingdom and his righteousness, and all these things will be given to you as well. Therefore do not worry about tomorrow, for tomorrow will worry about itself. Each day has enough trouble of its own.” (Matthew 6:31-34)

We don’t need to worry since Jesus will take care of our tomorrow. But we do need to seek His kingdom and His righteousness first and foremost in our lives, especially now in this critical hour. We do need to sink deep roots into our heavenly inheritance. His Kingdom is eternal. His Kingdom is unshakable. The stuff of this world is both temporary and shakable. We may be about to discover that more than ever, and it could be the very thing that causes us to sink deep roots in our eternal home.

I have been praying for revival for most of my adult life and I have studied the history of revivals. Most revivals have not come in times of ease, comfort and prosperity. Most revivals have come in times of famine, disease, difficulty, war and persecution. This current worldwide crisis may be the perfect birthing room for another historic awakening, if only the church can rise up to the occasion. Revival seldom comes on the heels of triumph but in the agony of defeat; it infrequently visits in times of prosperity and ease but in the pain of suffering. We stand on the precipice of a phenomenal kingdom moment.

Think about what happened in China when the church was persecuted, and the missionaries were kicked out. When China finally opened again and Christians from the West went back in, they were not sure what they would find. They were not convinced that the church would have been able to survive, but much to their surprise, they discovered the church did more than survive. The church exploded under the persecution and was expanding wildly. When the Vietnam war struck, the Christian and Missionary Alliance had to flee Vietnam. We pulled our missionaries out after several were martyred and, once again, we were not sure what we would discover when we returned to this persecuted church. But when the Western leaders of the C&MA went back into Vietnam, we discovered that the church had more than survived, it had exploded under the communist reign. The church in China and Vietnam went underground, they had to re-invent themselves, but the church prevailed. God redeemed the suffering and the Lord was adding daily to their numbers those who were being saved. The church rose to the occasion in those dark hours and the light the church shined became a hope to many and they reaped an unprecedented harvest.

In this short book, I don't just want to talk about how to survive a crisis or how to access the peace of God in the current chaos – we will address those things, but I want to go beyond that, beyond the self-focus of this season. I want to talk about how to capitalize off of a crisis to maximize momentum in the advance of the Kingdom of God. I want to talk about how you and I can grow through this crisis and become the people we need to be to seize the opportunity that will very likely soon be before us. We are poised to be in the right place at the right time for an unprecedented Kingdom opportunity, if only we can rise up to become the right people. People of faith not fear. People of courage, not cowardice. People who are generous, not hoarding. People who are deeply rooted in eternity, not overcome by too much attachment to the temporary. People of the Kingdom, not people of comfort. Together let's talk about how to become the right people so we can seize this ripe moment in Kingdom History. There is hope in Christ, and we need to dwell in it, and the world needs to discover it.

Chapter 1: The Unshakable Kingdom

When the horrified disciples woke Jesus from a blissful sleep in the midst of a terrifying storm, Jesus calmed the storm with a word, then He asked them, "Why are you so afraid? Do you still have no faith?" I have to confess that there are many times in my life where I think if I were face to face with Jesus, He would ask me the same questions. I think the questions we have to ask ourselves in return are, "Why did He expect that they would NOT be afraid? Why did He expect them to have faith?"

Jesus had just spent the entire chapter in Mark 4 teaching them about the Kingdom of God. He had explained to them that the Kingdom starts with small beginnings (like a mustard seed), but it has a certain and fruitful ending. It will grow; it will thrive! The Kingdom of God is not threatened by the circumstances of Earth because the Kingdom of God is eternal. Heaven is a superior realm to earth and therefore the Kingdom of God will prevail. Like the mustard seed that starts small, it will grow to become the largest of garden plants and become a refuge for weary travelers just as the birds take refuge in the shade of the mustard plant. The reason the disciples could have faith in their current crisis was because they were citizens of an unshakable Kingdom. How could they fear knowing that they were in the hands of a King whose Kingdom extended far beyond this world and was destined to prevail? If we are going to live free of fear in this world-changing moment of history, we are going to have to sink deep roots into our eternal Kingdom. Jesus expected His disciples to be so rooted in the eternal Kingdom, they would be unshakable in their temporal circumstances. If we are going to capitalize off of this moment in history, we are going to have to place greater stock in our heavenly home than our earthly comforts.

Fearless Citizens

The number one command in Scripture is "fear not"; this is the thing God says more often than anything else. I think God says this more often than He says anything else because fear makes us self-focused and selfish. In this current Coronavirus crisis that the world is undergoing, you have probably experienced the selfishness of fear. Recently, on a couple of occasions Jen and I went to the grocery store and there was no meat, no pasta, and no toilet paper or paper products. People are hoarding because of fear. Fear makes us focused on ourselves and inconsiderate of anyone else. In England the government pleaded with people to stop hoarding. They assured people that there would be enough for everyone, IF people stopped hoarding. But if they continued to hoard in fear, then some people would indeed be without. People still hoarded. Fear makes us selfish. But we follow the God of the cross. Jesus died on the cross in the most unselfish act in human history. We cannot be a light in the darkness or an anchor in the storm when we act in fear and follow our base instincts of selfishness. We cannot present the eternal hope of

Jesus effectively when our actions are marked by the fears of the temporal chaos.

Often, when we are afraid, it is because we are more focused on the temporal realities than we are on our eternal citizenship. In the book of Acts, the Apostle Paul is a force to be reckoned with in the Kingdom of God. His earthly effectiveness is directly connected to his eternal certainty. In Philippians 1, Paul runs into a unique problem. He has some opponents who are preaching the gospel just to stir up trouble for him. Paul is in prison, but he isn't bothered by their disingenuous antics. He says, "But what does it matter? The important thing is that in every way, whether from false motives or true, Christ is preached. And because of this I rejoice" (Philippians 1:18). You gotta love this guy! He understands the stakes. Their actions produced from false motives could lead to further persecution. It could even lead to his death, but he is unphased by the earthly possibilities because he is focused on his eternal certainties in Christ. He is focused on the advance of the gospel of the Kingdom, not his personal situation, safety or security. This is what makes him an unstoppable force in the Kingdom. It isn't his gifts, talents or abilities; it isn't his brilliance, wisdom or strategic intent; it is his certainty in the superior realm of heaven that thrusts him forward as a light in the darkness. He isn't fearful, selfish or temporal in his outlook; He is courageous, Kingdom-oriented and unstoppable in his eternal insight.

He tells the church at Philippi that he expects he will be delivered from his current dilemma with the help of their prayers, but he is fine either way. And then this line: "For to me, to live is Christ and to die is gain" (Philippians 1:21). No, really, pause and read that again. Take that line in. Paul is so clear in his mind about the eternal realities of heaven that he believes it is actually better for him to die than it is for him to live. That's faith at its very best, at its most commendable, at its most powerful, at its most unstoppable. He truly believes that there is more to be gained in death than there is in life. How do you stop this man? What can you do to a person who has such a mindset? He goes on to say to them: "If I am to go on living in the body, this will mean fruitful labor for me. Yet what shall I choose? I do not know! I am torn between the two: I desire to depart and be with Christ, which is better by far; but it is more necessary for you that I remain in the body. Convinced of this, I know that I will remain, and I will continue with all of you for your progress and joy in the faith" (Philippians 1:22-25).

Paul's roots in eternity go so deep, the current crisis of his life cannot shake him. He is like an oak tree so deeply and securely rooted that it remains standing even in the worst of storms. No matter what the outcome, he is convinced that Jesus will win, and he will be fine because he is in Christ. His attachment to heaven is so real, the threat of any detachment from earthly comforts – even life itself – does not shake him. He tells this church later in the letter, "Our citizenship is in heaven. And we eagerly await a Savior from there, the Lord Jesus Christ, who by the power that enables him to bring everything under his control, will transform our lowly bodies so that they will be like his glorious body" (Philippians 3:20-21).

I've heard it said of some people that they are so heavenly minded they are no earthly good. But I'm not convinced of that. It is more likely that they are so religiously molded, they are no earthly or heavenly good. But true heavenly mindedness produces the most earthly good, because it makes us fearless in crisis, courageous for the Kingdom, and passionate for the cause of Christ. Paul is an unstoppable force for the Kingdom because of his singular heavenly mindedness. He labors for heaven; he lives for Jesus and His eternal kingdom. His focus is unmovable. His passion is unshakable. He has nothing to lose on earth; if they kill him, he gains heaven and gets to be with Jesus! If they let him live, He does more to advance the Kingdom so that many others can get to know Jesus. Either way, the Kingdom of Heaven benefits because of his focused, eternal mindset. We would sincerely benefit from a lot more heavenly mindedness in our current situation.

It may be that the current crisis makes us more heavenly minded. It is quite possible that this is the very thing we need to shake our confidence in our earthly goods, resources, comforts and plans. The threat of death may make us more attached to our eternal life. The loss of comforts may make us more comforted by our eternal inheritance.

Unshakable Kingdom

In Hebrews 12, the author compares the kingdoms of this world, with the eternal Kingdom of God. The kingdoms of this world will all be shaken out. It is like a small throw rug that we pick up and take outside and shake it to get the dirt out of it. So, God will shake out the kingdoms of this world. All of the kingdoms will come to an end. All of the wealth is temporary and cannot be carried with us into the next world. All of the earthly comforts will be removed. None of it will last. Hebrews 12:26f, "At that time his voice shook the earth, but now he has promised, 'Once more I will shake not only the earth but also the heavens.' The words 'once more' indicate the removing of what can be shaken – that is, created things – so that what cannot be shaken may remain." In the end, everything that is temporary will be removed and only the eternal will be left standing. All who hope in the temporary things will be disappointed. Only the things that we do with a heavenly mindset, with an eternal motivation, will remain. Our houses, our bank accounts, our possessions, our jobs, and all of the visible aspects of this world will be shaken out. They will not last. They are not secure. Therefore, they cannot offer security, hope or lasting comfort. They are temporal; therefore, they cannot bring you lasting joy.

The problem is that we often become more attached to these temporal things than we do to the eternal Kingdom. They are tangible and feel more real than the eternal things – until they are threatened. We put our hope and our trust in these things and derive our comfort from these things while we are here on earth. But when we go through a time like this when all of our temporary securities are threatened, we shake in fear over them as they are shaken out. But then the eternal things come into focus and the unshakable things become our foundation.

The author goes on to say, "Therefore, since we are receiving a kingdom that cannot be shaken, let us be thankful, and so worship God acceptably with reverence and awe, for our 'God is a consuming fire'" (Hebrews 12:28-29). In chapter 13 he leads us to the implications of being part of an unshakable Kingdom. In v.6 he says, "So we say with confidence, 'The Lord is my helper; I will not be afraid. What can human beings do to me?'" Brilliant! This is what Paul understood.

Paul understood that his health and his earthly body were merely part of this very shakable, completely destructible, temporary world. If he was persecuted, he would be rewarded in heaven for his earthly suffering. If he was martyred, he would be promoted to heaven, get to be with Jesus and come into his eternal inheritance and receive his heavenly body that would be indestructible. If he died in prison, he would awake in heaven in the arms of Jesus. One day, no matter how it came, his human existence would be shaken out, he would breathe his last breath, and he would be shaken out - just like all of the rest of the temporary things in this world – wealth, belongings, and positions. The only thing that would be left would be what he did for Jesus – to live is Christ, to die is gain.

When I was in second grade we moved to a new house. The new house didn't have a lawn yet, so my brother and I worked with my Dad to put in the lawn. We ordered countless truckloads of topsoil and spread it across the existing landfill dirt that couldn't grow grass. But before we could spread it over the yard, we had to sift it because it had sticks and stones and hard clumps of dirt in it. We sifted all of the topsoil by hand. We threw shovelfuls of dirt on top of a steel mesh grate and we moved it back and forth until the good dirt fell through the grid. We collected the soft, refined topsoil and spread it. We took the stones, the sticks, and the other debris that was left and we threw it in a back corner of the property as part of the landfill. One day this world will be sifted out, and only that which is done for the eternal Kingdom will survive. We don't want to get attached to the sticks, and stones and debris of this temporary planet that will be sifted out; we only want attachment to the pure goods of the Kingdom.

Detachment

The old timers used to talk about 'detachment.' They challenged us to detach from earthly things in order to more securely attach to the heavenly King and His Kingdom. This is what they understood: The problem with too much earthly attachment is that it robs us of our heavenly affection and our eternal effectiveness. Jesus said, "Do not store up for yourselves treasures on earth, where moth and rust destroy, and where thieves break in and steal. But store up for yourselves treasures in heaven, where moth and rust do not destroy, and where thieves do not break in and steal. For where your treasure is, there you heart will be also" (Matthew 6:19-21). If I have my attachments and comforts in the here and now, my heavenly affection will be dulled. Earth bound attachment prevents us from making Jesus our first love. If we are going to have a pure, undivided love for Jesus, sifting is necessary. Crisis creates sifting; sifting creates unadulterated attachments to Jesus.

In comfort-based societies, it is virtually impossible not to have some earthbound attachment taking up space in our hearts. But seasons like this Coronavirus that we are currently confronting sift us. They have the capacity to separate us from our earthly attachments, which create temporal affections, and rob us of our eternal focus.

John Wesley noticed this phenomenon in the First Great Awakening. Many of the people who came to faith in Christ were poor and were engaged in wasted self-indulgence. Often, for example, they would drink to drown out some of the difficulties of their life which created more economic hardships for them. When they came to Christ, they often had a change of priorities and it caused them to clean up their lives and change their behaviors. They experienced what Wesley called, 'redemption and lift.' After they came to Christ, they gave up drunkenness and other nefarious activities. They also became more industrious as their lives were marked with more meaning. This led them to experience an economic lift; the result was that they had more money. But the economic lift often threatened their newfound passion for Jesus because they became more attached to temporal things and it robbed their heart's affections and threatened to snuff out their new spiritual fire. Wesley said the only solution was the more they made, the more they had to give; they more they gave, the more they invested their treasure and heart in heaven. They had to detach from the temporary and attach to the eternal. Where their treasure was, their heart would be. They had to intentionally invest in eternity.

I have had to cancel conferences that I was scheduled to speak at because of the social distancing. Currently, as I write, four months' worth of conferences have been canceled. Between the honorarium and the books that I would sell at these conferences it will cost me tens of thousands of dollars. Yet the bills still have to be paid. And it has stirred some fear in me. I didn't actually feel fear; I felt irritated. One day Jen said to me, "Are you irritated with me?" I wasn't. But as I sat with the Lord over my irritation and the vibrations within my soul, I knew it was fear lurking deep within the corridors of my heart. And I had to be honest with God and myself that the fear was there because I had put some trust in my ability to make money, in my income and my comforts. I like the comforts of modern society. I like the benefits of having more than enough. I like having money in my savings, and a sense of security from my hopeful retirement plans. I want to know that there is enough for Jen if I should suddenly die. Money creates options, and options are more appealing in life. But those things can create some level of comfort and security which are rooted in the temporal; they are earthly treasures that form earthly attachments and when they are threatened our souls rumble with fear and angst.

There is nothing as effective as a heavenly sifting to help you detach from earthly treasures and develop newfound security in your heavenly home. When these earthly attachments are threatened to be dislodged from our grip, we have a divine opportunity to strengthen our heavenly attachments and renew our affections for Jesus. So, I have been surrendering earthly attachments and comforts these days. I have been dying to self once again and recommitting myself to my eternal citizenship.

Jesus: Our First Affection

Jesus told us we didn't have to worry about what we would eat or drink or wear. He said, like the birds of the air, the Father would care for us too. But He ended that section of the Sermon on the Mount with these words, "But seek first his kingdom and his righteousness, and all these things will be given to you as well." We don't have to worry, but we do have to put the eternal things of God first. The King and his Kingdom must pre-occupy our hearts. If we put the eternal things of God first, we won't worry – because where our treasure is, our hearts will be. But when our security is derived from our earthly comforts, when they are threatened, we will worry. Our worry is a byproduct of our attachments.

So, this is a divine opportunity for us to allow the Master Teacher to shape our hearts and to realign our priorities. Let's give Him access. Let's give him permission to detach our earthly comforts. Let's confess that we have trusted too much in our earthly treasures. And let's commit ourselves afresh to put his Kingdom first and seek a purity, a righteousness, an alignment with God's ways and doings. Let's surrender ourselves to the King, so we can get about his eternal Kingdom business with renewed passion and fresh focus. Let's give ourselves wholeheartedly to the King, so that He is our unqualified and unchallenged number one affection. Revival cannot take place where Jesus is not the first love of our hearts. Revival, by necessity, must challenge all other competitors to Jesus' pre-eminent position in the human heart. When Jesus is our first love, revival is beginning within us. Where our earthly attachments numb our heavenly affections for Jesus, we need to detach in order to renew those affections. This is a Kingdom moment for the church to purify her heart and sink deep roots into her eternal citizenship.

When Jen and I first moved to the South Shore of Boston, we were passionate about building relationships with people who didn't know Christ, so that everyone could experience the reality of Jesus' love and the security of their heavenly home. One day Jen was out hanging laundry on our fence in the backyard of the parsonage where we lived. As she went to slip a rope over the fence post so she could hang the laundry, an old woman came out on her back porch and yelled at Jen: "Hey! Get that rope off of my fence post! You can't hang that there!" Jen was stunned by the rebuke. At the same time an old guy directly in back of our house came out on his back porch and shouted at the old woman, "Old bitty, go inside! Leave her alone!" The old woman slinked back into her house, and the old guy told Jen she could hang her rope on his fence post. That unique interaction introduced us to Bud, our backyard neighbor.

Over the next few weeks we talked to Bud across the fence and then one day we invited him to our house for dinner. He dressed up and came over – later I found out that it was the first time he went to someone's house for dinner in four decades! He was an old curmudgeon and we loved him. He started attending church with us; he even started giving money away to the church as his affections began to shift from the temporal to the eternal.

One day he called me up on the phone and asked me to come over to his house. He was deeply disturbed. When I got there, he told me about a dream that he had the night before. In the dream he was standing on his back porch and he saw his wife in the backyard. She had died many years earlier. He said to her, "Oh, Gerry, it's so good to see you. I've missed you." In the dream, she said to him, "You'll see me soon." The dream terrified him because he was afraid to die. Bud said to me, "I've lived a selfish life; I've wasted my life living for myself. I'm not ready to die and face the judgment." I explained to him that none of us get to go to heaven on our own merit. That's why Jesus came. He was tempted in every way we are, but He never sinned. Then He died on the cross, in our place. He died and took up our sins on the cross, so that our hearts and souls can be washed clean and we can be made acceptable to God. Jesus then rose and conquered death, and all who trust in Him will overcome death with Him and they will live forever. "I am the resurrection and the life. Anyone who believes in me will live, even though they die; and whoever lives believing in me will never die" (John 11:25-26). Bud prayed with me. I prayed that the Holy Spirit would give him peace, so that he would no longer be afraid to die. And the peace came.

I came home from that encounter and I told Jen about the dream he had, and I said to her, "Bud is going to die. The Lord is preparing him for his death; so that he can die in peace." I knew the dream was from the Lord. A couple of weeks later he went into the hospital for a routine surgery. I drove him in. I visited him in the hospital. The day he was supposed to come home from the hospital he woke up and got dressed. Bud's son was coming to drive him home and stay with him during the recovery period. The nurse came in and helped him get ready. She cheerfully said to him, "Today is the day you get to go home, Mr. Alden." He responded equally cheerfully, "Nope. Today is the day I am going to die." She said, "Oh, no, Mr. Alden. You're confused. Today is the day you are going home. Your son is coming to pick you up. Remember?" He smiled and said, "Nope. Today is the day I'm going to die." And a little less than an hour later he died in the hospital suddenly to everyone's surprise – except for me, Bud and the Lord.

He died in peace because he died to his self-centered living, he detached from his earthly comforts and attached to the unshakable Kingdom and the unstoppable King. Herein lies all hope. You can rest in peace for eternity because Jesus has conquered death. You can rest in peace in the current crisis, no matter how it turns out, because Jesus has secured your eternal home. You are just passing through. All of this will be shaken out. But you are part of an unshakable Kingdom. Sink deep roots and rest in peace whether you live or die. For it is true that for us, to live is Christ and to die is gain.

Chapter 2: Overcoming Fear

Show me how a person handles a crisis and it will tell me a lot about the person's interior life. *Crises reveal the cracks in the interior walls of our soul. Crises don't create inner problems; crises reveal inner problems*. This is why crises are often a great opportunity to deal with our issues and experience transformation. It was a marriage crisis that led me down the road of inner healing; it led me to discover how to appropriate the victories of Jesus for freedom in my life. It literally changed my life and saved my marriage. I wouldn't have gone after the broken places in my soul if it had not been for that crisis. Crises often become opportunities because they expose us to our weak spots that need God's transforming and fortifying strength and power. Crises lead us out of the illusion of independence and back to the reality of our utter dependence on God.

This particular world crisis is revealing cracks in most of our souls. Fear is being exposed. Though some of you, like me, may not feel fear – you may feel irritable or angry. Often for Type A personalities, fear shows up with power emotions like anger. We are discovering that we have had more attachments to health, and comforts than we may have realized. Thus, the threat to our health and comfortable lifestyles creates fear. But this is a golden opportunity for us to process our inner issues so that we can become the kind of people God can use in an increasingly significant worldwide catastrophe. Only people who are deeply rooted in their eternal realities can make a significant impact for the Kingdom of God in this temporary world.

Let's look at some really practical help in overcoming fear. Even if you are wrestling with some of the side effects of fear like irritability, anger, or control, you must deal with the disease, not the symptoms in order to gain the victory. We must go after the root, not the fruit. Fear is a primary emotion. This is why the Lord says, "Fear not," more than He says anything else in the Bible. He knew that this primary emotion could do irreparable damage to our spiritual lives if we didn't go after it.

Take Responsible Action

First, if we are going to overcome fear, we need to begin by doing what we can do. Fear often paralyzes us. We feel overwhelmed, helpless and defeated and we sometimes fail to act on what we can do. The people of Israel came to the brink of the Promised Land and fearful inaction won the day. Moses sent spies into the land – two came back and talked about the land's bounty, but ten came back and reported that there were giants in the land and that they would be annihilated. Fear ruled. The people refused to act. They refused to do what God told them to do – God told them that He would provide the victory; God had promised the land to them. But their fear made them turn away from their part which was to act in obedient faith. They refused to take responsible action and step into the land and trust God for the victory He had promised.

Fear caused an entire generation of people to miss out on their prophetic destiny. This was the PROMISED LAND. God had promised it to them; it was their inheritance. But they missed out on their inheritance, they were robbed of their prophetic destiny because of fear. When fear paralyzes us, we miss out on the opportunities before us. *When fear paralyzes us, we forfeit divine promises and forgo kingdom opportunities.* So, don't get paralyzed in fear but step out in obedient faith to do what God is asking you to do in this season. Do what you can do.

In our case, long before COVID-19 came, Jen decided last year to quit her job and come to work with me full time in the ministry, Renewal International. The vast majority of our income comes from the conferences that I lead and the books that I sell in those conferences. In an effort to stop the spread of the Coronavirus, group gatherings have been halted. All of my conferences for at least the next four months have been canceled. As I said, it will literally cost Jen and I tens of thousands of dollars' worth of income and as a result we won't have sufficient funds coming in the house to pay our bills. I felt fear like many others and then I determined I needed to do what I could. I am going to try livestream conferences, something I've never done before. Will it work? I don't know, especially since people tend to spend less in times of crisis as expected. But that's the way I make my living, so I am doing what I can do. By the way, we ran our first conference and it paid the bills for the first month – so far, so good.

Psalm 62 is one of my favorite Psalms. Verse 1 says, "For God alone my soul waits in silence; from Him comes my salvation" (ESV). Sometimes you have done everything you can do, you have said everything you can say, you have prayed everything you can pray, and all that is left to do is wait upon the Lord. But before we wait and do nothing – let's make sure we have done what we can do, said what we can say and prayed what we can pray. Let's do our part, then let's wait for God to do His part.

Hold on to God's Love

Second, position yourself to receive and hold on to the love of God. John said, "And so we know and rely on the love God has for us. God is love. Whoever lives in love lives in God, and God in them. This is how love is made complete among us so that we have confidence on the day of judgment: In this world we are like Jesus. There is no fear in love. But perfect love drives out fear, because fear has to do with punishment. The one who fears is not made perfect in love" (1 John 4:16-18).

We begin by holding on to what we know to be true. We know God is love. We know God loves us because of the cross. We know John 3:16 that reminds us that God proved his great love for us through Jesus' life and death. We remind ourselves of this and we hold on to the truth that the Scriptures makes plain to us. But John calls us out beyond the boundaries of knowledge and into deep dependence. "We rely on the love God has for us." Knowledge can get you by in good times, but in times of crisis knowledge doesn't run deep enough to hold us firm. When the foundations are shaking, we need more than knowledge. We need to learn how to rely on God's love. We need revelation. *The great gap in our Christian lives is often the gap between what we know and what has not yet been made known to us through the revelation of the Holy Spirit.* In times like this we are forced to rely on God's love. It becomes something we go to again and again as we learn to hold on to the truth. We sit with God in silence while we hold on to this truth and God takes that which we know, and He makes it known to our inner beings. He reveals the truth to our souls through revelation and He makes it personal.

We hold on to love while we are fighting for victory over fear and God reveals His love to us in our morning time with Him. But by the evening, we have lost our grip on love and we come back to God again and we hold on to love again. And God reveals His love to us once again. Often in times of crisis we learn to lean into the love of God moment by moment. I learned this during my marriage crisis. And God delivered. He gave me enough moment by moment love to hold on, to get through, to learn that his love was dependable and unshakable. Learning to depend on God's love and rely on God's love is a process of relentlessly returning to the One who loves us and receiving what we need for the moment at hand. The more we return to receive it, the more He releases and reveals it, the deeper it settles into our core.

In those darkest days of my marriage crisis, every night Jen and I would discuss the things that were problematic in our marriage. She was angry and she was trying to articulate what had hurt her. Every night after our time of discussion, I would go upstairs to be alone with God and process the things Jen had shared with me. I was restless with fear – my mind was racing and my heart was anxious. I often took an hour just to soak in the love of God. I listened to worship songs about God's love, I meditated on Scripture about God's love, I listened to the Holy Spirit's whispers about God's love. I was learning to rely on God's love, to settle the love of God deeper into my soul. After I had secured my soul in the certain love of Christ, then I would bring the things Jen said to me before the Lord. I would own whatever the Lord told me I needed to own. And I would end my time by asking myself this question: *How would a deeply loved person act right now?* I was learning to rely on God's love. The next night, I would have to do it all over again. The stronger the fear, the more frequently you need to reposition the love of God at the center of your soul. But you must act on the love you have received, not on the fear that seizes your heart. Only as we act on love do we learn to rely on love.

While we are holding on to the love of God and He is making it known to us, we must live it out. "Whoever lives in love lives in God, and God in them." Often, when we are hunkering down in fear, we don't live out God's love. Generosity dries up, for example, in times of crisis like COVID-19 because we are paralyzed by fear and we stop giving. Generosity flows from a heart that is secure in love. Generosity can only flow from a heart that is secure – if we are secure in our abundance, we may be generous while we still feel safe in our abundance, but the moment our abundance is threatened we will stop being generous. That is because our security came from our abundance of temporal wealth, and not from the abundance of God's eternal love. Christian generosity must be rooted in the abundant love of God that secures us to our heavenly home and allows us to detach from our earthly possessions. We can give away that which we are not dependent upon for our security.

As we learn to rely on the love of God, we must learn to live like Jesus, love like Jesus, act like Jesus, give like Jesus, and serve like Jesus. We can do this because the same Spirit that lived in Jesus lives in us and the Spirit pours out the love of God in our hearts (Romans 5). God is love. His source of love never dries up. There is plenty; there is no scarcity of love in the heart of God. Living out the love that we receive gives us confidence, John says, on the day of judgment because in this world we are like Jesus.

John makes an extraordinary statement: "There is no fear in love. But perfect love drives out fear, because fear has to do with punishment. The one who fears is not made perfect in love" (1 John 4:18). There is no fear in love – when we still are afraid, we have not been made perfect in love. Wow. Hold on to that. Linger with that for a moment. Fear has to do with punishment – fear that I will not be enough, do enough, have enough. Fear that I don't measure up; I won't be acceptable or accepted. Fear that I don't belong. Fear that my sins will not be forgotten, and my good deeds will not be sufficient. I have often talked to Christians who are afraid that if they mess up, God is going to punish them. I have talked to Christ-followers who believe that their life is hard because God is punishing them. Life is hard because life is life. We live in a fallen, broken, sin-stained planet. Life is not hard because God's love is deficient in any way.

I believe in the discipline of the Lord. It is Scriptural, but if you read Hebrews 12 it is clear that the discipline of the Lord is restorative, not punitive. God doesn't punish us in a vengeful way when we do wrong; God corrects our wayward paths because He loves us like a good Father, and He wants to restore us. Only when we are in alignment with Him can we have abundant life. This mindset of a punitive Father is not a mindset that is mature in love; it is a mindset of an infantile understanding of the love of God in Christ. "The one who fears is not made perfect in love." *When fear has a grip on us, we have lost our grip on God's love. But even then, God's love has not lost its grip on us.*

Use this season in your life to be made perfect in love. Hold on to the truth. Learn to rely on God's love in this current crisis – day by day, moment by moment. Meditate on Scriptures that speak of God's love. Let the Holy Spirit bring illumination to the truth you know, so that it may be made known in the deep places in your heart. Sit alone with the Spirit of God in stillness and let Him witness to your inner being and testify to you about the love of the Father. Paul talks about this reality in Romans 8:14-17, "For those who are led by the Spirit of God are the children of God. The Spirit you received does not make you slaves, so that you live in fear again; rather, the Spirit you received brought about your adoption to sonship. And by him we cry, 'Abba, Father.' The Spirit himself testifies with our spirit that we are God's children." You have been adopted into the family of God because of the unrelenting love of your Father in Heaven and the Spirit of God is working overtime to let you know deep within your heart that you are dearly loved. We have to make room for the Spirit to speak to our inner beings, and we have to hold on to the truth He makes known to us. As love is made perfect in you, let love shine through you. Step out in faith and live a life of love. Extend the love of God to those around you.

Set our Hearts on Eternity

Third, if we are going to overcome fear, we need to remember the King and his eternal Kingdom. Times of crisis cause us to fix our eyes on the problems and the temporal which only aggravates our fear. The problems consume space in our minds and hearts, and we become preoccupied with the circumstances. *Worry is a preoccupation with our problems; peace is a byproduct of our fixation on Jesus. We have to set our hearts on the eternal.*

Paul said, "Since, then, you have been raised with Christ, set your hearts on things above, where Christ is seated at the right hand of God. Set your minds on things above, not on earthly things. For you died, and your life is now hidden with Christ in God. When Christ, who is your life, appears, then you also will appear with him in glory" (Colossians 3:1f). Set your hearts on things above – set your affections on heaven and the things that matter forever. Use Scripture and worship and thanksgiving to set your hearts on things above. Meditate on passages about your eternal home, your heavenly citizenship. Sing songs that fix your heart on Jesus and his heavenly Kingdom. Give God thanks for all of the good things you have in Christ.

Set your minds on things above. Times of crisis are opportunities for purgation that allow us to more thoroughly align ourselves with God. At the end of this, won't it be best if the things that matter to God matter more to you? When people come to the end of their life, they don't care about how much money they have or the positions they held or the possessions they cherished. When people come to the end of their days, they think about the people that matter most; they think about what happens after they die. They think about what they have done to contribute to God's Kingdom or to leave a legacy. When I am tempted with fear in this season, I take time to think of Jesus on his throne seated in the heavenly realms at the right hand of God. He isn't nervous. He isn't ringing his hands in heaven wondering how in the world He is going to get us out of this mess. He is at peace. He has compassion, but He hasn't lost his peace. Then I think about my position in Christ. I am in Christ; Christ is in me. I belong. I am loved. I am His. I think about dying. When I die, the coronavirus isn't going to worry me. The economic state of the world is not going to preoccupy my thoughts. And I intentionally set my heart and my mind on the things above and on the One who is fully worthy of my whole heart's affections. If I lose my peace again later in the day, I do it again. And again. And again. Because though I lose my perspective, He has not lost His.

Cling to the Promises of God

Fourth, if we are going to overcome these fearful times and seize the Kingdom opportunity before us, then we need to cling to the promises of God. *The promises of God have always seen the people of God through the most impossible circumstances in the most improbable ways.* Some of the promises of God are straight from the Word; others may come to you directly from the Spirit. Matthew 6, as we looked at earlier, promises that God will provide for our basic needs if we put His Kingdom first. Most of the promises of God are conditional like that – if you seek His kingdom and His righteousness, then He will provide. We have to do our part before we can claim His part. This is a time to take Him seriously, and get ourselves into alignment with our part, and then vigilantly claim His promises.

Can't we claim the promise that God will provide in times like these if we go all in for Jesus and His cause? We can't claim big houses, fancy cars and all of the comforts that we may have become used to, but we can claim provision for our needs. We can hold on to the promises in His Word. Jen and I might have to downsize. We might not be able to ever retire. I might have to do interim pastorates into my later years, but if we put God first, God promised to provide. I can believe Him for that provision and when I stop focusing on my present problems and focus on His prevailing promises, I feel his peace. I have prayed for revival my whole life and I would rather lose everything and see it come than hold on to my comforts and miss it. So, if God can redeem this to bring about another great awakening, then I am willing to hold on to His promise that He can provide for me in the midst of all the chaos.

I am going to hold on to the promise that His Kingdom is unstoppable – it will prevail. In Mark 4, Jesus said the Kingdom of God is like a mustard seed and it may start small, but it will grow, and it will be a refuge for many. In Matthew 16, Jesus promised that the church will prevail, and the gates of hell will not overcome it (Mt 16:18). It is an unshakable Kingdom (Hebrews 12:26-29) and your citizenship in this unshakable Kingdom is secure (Phil 3:20-21). Hold on to these promises. They can stabilize you in shaky times.

When you claim the promises of God, make sure you pray in faith and not in fear. Often, I hear people claiming promises, but I can tell they are praying them out of their fears. The problem is when we pray in fear, we reinforce the fear at the center of our being. So, take the time to get your eyes on Jesus, strengthen your grip on eternity, set your mind and heart on things above, and then pray in faith with authority.

Deny Ourselves

Fifth, if we are going to overcome fear and seize this moment in Kingdom history, then we are going to have to die to self. Fear gets our eyes off of God and onto ourselves. Fear makes us self-focused and selfish; we become hoarders with a scarcity mindset, rather than generous givers with a sacrificial mindset like Jesus. We have to die to our fears. We have to die to our rights to have abundance, to have certain comforts. We have to die to our attachments to our earthly possessions and positions. *Jesus called us into death, so He could give us life.* Jesus didn't come to be served, but to give His life away as ransom. Jesus called us to follow Him on the way to the cross: "Whoever wants to be my disciple must deny themselves and take up their cross daily and follow me" (Luke 9:23).

I have discovered in my life that nearly every time I am miserable, I am making it too much about me. I wish that were not true, but it is. When I am miserable in marriage, I am making it too much about me. I am making it about my rights, my needs, my wants, and my desires. I have to die to self to get free from misery. When I am upset over my finances, I am almost always making it too much about me. I am comparing myself to someone else. I am looking at what I have and what they have and I am feeling slighted or cheated or envious. It is unfair. But the moment I can stop making it about me, the moment I take up my cross and die to self, the moment I take my eyes off of me and put them back on Jesus, the misery lifts from my soul. *Death to self is the path to life. If you want to live the abundant life in Christ, you must die to your miserable self-life.* That is never more true than when we are tempted by fear to become self-focused.

Part of dying to self is not giving yourself permission to obsess. When we are fearful our minds get stuck like an old record with a skip and we entertain the same thoughts over and over again. We get caught in a doom loop and we can't get out. We keep thinking about our finances or our health or whatever we are fearful about. Dying to self means that I don't give myself permission to keep thinking about those things. I give God thanks for His promise, I hold on to His promise, I meditate on Scripture about His love, but I move my thoughts off of self and onto God. I bow my stiff neck and die to my self-centered focus. I make it about the King and His Kingdom.

Face the Worst with Faith

Sixth, if we are going to overcome our fears and seize this kingdom moment before us, we must face the worst possibilities with faith. Don't get me wrong. I am not talking about obsessing over the worst possibilities; we need to die to fear-based obsessive thoughts. But I do think we need to face the reality of the hard times that are before us. I have to steel myself to face those potential difficulties with faith. I play 'worst case scenario.' What is the worst-case scenario? What is the worst thing that can happen here? Physically? I could get COVID-19 and die. Then I go to heaven and I get to meet Jesus face to face and I get my resurrection body that is indestructible. I am ready and I am with Paul – to die is gain. I'm not rushing it, but if Jesus calls me home, I am excited about that possibility. Home. Home to heaven where there is no more sickness, no more death, no more heartache, no more suffering, no more struggle, no more painful human interactions, no more battle against sin, temptation and evil. Home. To a place of perfect peace, perfect love, perfect harmony. Yup. I'm ready; that's not so bad. And I can trust Jesus to take care of the family that I left behind. That's the worst-case scenario – and not likely for me at this point. So, why worry?

What's the worst that can happen financially? I could lose all source of income and have to depend on God for everyday provision, for my daily bread, in the midst of a worldwide economic catastrophe. I have to say this doesn't appeal to me. Heaven sounds better than this. I have grown accustomed to having enough – enough food, enough money, enough stuff. And I have grown up in America – in a land of plenty. I've never had to think about my next meal or being able to pay my basic bills. I don't really want to live through economic deprivation, if I am really honest. But God can redeem it in my life. He can provide and He can teach me dependence and draw me closer to Him through that kind of living. He takes care of the birds of the air and they don't sweat it. He can take care of me and my family – day by day, He can provide. And I can learn to depend on Him for daily provision and I can become more dependent on Him than ever before; my faith can expand greatly in such dependence.

My grandparents lived through the Great Depression. I remember sitting around and asking my grandparents about it when I got older. No one loved it. Those were hard times. But when I talked to my grandmother about it, she recalled it with fondness. She talked to me about God's miraculous provisions. She spoke of neighbors doing acts of kindness to help you get by – an act of kindness that you often had opportunity to return later on. God came through and people came together. *Hard times are often times when small kindnesses become great blessings and things that were taken for granted are experienced with sincere gratitude.* Life is short. This too will pass, no matter how dark it gets and God will see us through. So, let's face the hardships with the faith that we have a good Father who provides for His children and has prepared a place for them and one day will call them Home.

Paul faced the worst with faith in Acts 21 when Agabus came to him and took his belt and bound his hands and said, "In this way the Jewish leaders in Jerusalem will bind the owner of this belt and will hand him over to the Gentiles" (Acts 21:11). Paul's friends pleaded with him not to go through with his plans. But Paul answered, "Why are you weeping and breaking my heart? I am ready not only to be bound, but also to die in Jerusalem for the name of the Lord Jesus" (Acts 21:13). What's the worst case? I can die. Ok, I'm willing for the Lord Jesus!

Esther did this too. When Mordecai persuaded her to help the desperate situation of the Jews by approaching the King, she faced the reality that approaching the King without his explicit invitation could lead to her execution. She signed on for her tough assignment and she approached the king to have mercy on her people anyway. She faced the worst possible scenario with faith as she said to Mordecai, "If I perish, I perish." Worst case? I die. Ok, I can face that with faith - for such a time as this.

Face the Worst with Redemptive Hope

Lastly, if we are going to overcome our fear and seize this kingdom moment, then we must face the worst scenario with the best possible redemptive outcomes. Sure, it could be the worst of times, but maybe it could also be the best of times too – as Dickens said. What could God do to redeem these times in your life, in the church and in the world? Thinking about God's redeeming work lets me face a crisis with hope and even anticipation. It feeds my faith and makes me pray with an eternal focus. What if these very dark times could be redeemed in God's eternal scheme for the saving of countless lives? Would you be willing to endure difficulty for that? Would you be willing to face these hard times with faith – for such a time as this? What if they led you to strip away earthly attachments and purified you to enter into a new level of intimacy with God? What if it became more about His presence and less about His presents?

Recently I was thinking about two other Biblical characters who demonstrated unique faith. The first is Caleb. Caleb and Joshua believed God for the Promised Land the first time around, but their generation didn't. The people were ruled by fear and missed their historic kingdom moment. But after that first generation wandered around for forty years and finally died off, Joshua and Caleb were still around. Moses was gone; Joshua was leading the people into the land and Caleb came to Joshua to discuss his portion of the land. This is what Caleb said, "Now then, just as the Lord promised, he has kept me alive for forty-five years since the time he said this to Moses, while Israel moved about in the wilderness. So here I am today, eighty-five years old! I am still as strong as the day Moses sent me out. I am just as vigorous to go out to battle now as I was then." (Joshua 14:10f)

You've got to love this guy! What he is saying is completely not true, but it is a great perspective! Come on! He is eighty-five years old; he is not as strong as he was at forty. Can't you picture his troops in back of him going, "Come on Gramps! Get a grip!" They are probably picturing battle scenes in their mind – "Hey Pops! That guy is getting away – hit him with your cane! There goes another one – trip him with your staff before he gets by you!" He is not as strong as he was. This isn't the perspective of reality; this is the perspective of faith! *This is what happens when faith gets mingled with your current crisis, and you see things from God's perspective. You see redemptive possibilities.* This isn't the perspective of his circumstances; this is the perspective of the promises of God. He is holding on to the promise for the Promised Land nearly five decades later.

This is what we need today in the midst of this world crisis. We need people of faith who see these circumstances through the lens of God's promises. We need people who see the redemptive possibilities to cast visions of hope for all who have ears to hear.

Then think with me about John, the apostle. I was reading John 20 this week. Mary Magdalene and some women come to the tomb only to discover the stone is rolled away and Jesus is missing. They wonder who has stolen the body and they run to get

Peter and John. John outran Peter to the tomb, and he looks in, but waits for Peter. Peter goes in and he wonders what has happened (Luke 24:12). But John goes in, sees the grave clothes and puts it together. "He saw and believed" (John 20:8). John came expecting to find a grave robbery because the women told him that someone had stolen the body, but when he saw the grave clothes, he knew this was no robbery. Why would someone steal the body and take the time to take off his clothes? And when that occurs to him, I suspect the words of Jesus came back to him – that he must be crucified and after three days rise again. And John believed. The women wondered who stole the body. Peter wondered what happened. But John saw and believed.

Both Caleb and John are early adopters of deep faith. They believe when no one else believes. They see what God is doing before anyone else sees. They trust God to do the impossible before anyone else trusts. They see redemptive possibilities when everyone else only sees the problems. They have faith to seize a Kingdom moment.

We have an opportunity to be early adopters of faith and to become part of a new movement of God's Kingdom. We can act on fear and let our fears rule us, or we can believe like Caleb and John and see the story that God is writing before anyone else sees. We can be part of what God is doing in our generation!

Chapter 3: Drawing Near to God

Hardship has often been a catalyst to new depths of intimacy with God in my life. This has been the testimony of many of the saints throughout the ages. It is often during seasons of difficulty and pain that we lean into God in whole new ways. We develop dependence; we deepen trust. We draw near to God's heart. We discover new facets of God's goodness. We find out about the faithfulness of God in action. We experience more of His redeeming power and rejuvenating presence. We discover things about ourselves too – areas we need to surrender, sins we need to confess, truths we need to apply, wounds we need to heal, bondage we need to break, and freedom we need to access.

Think about your own journey: I am certain that most of you can look to seasons of hardship in your life that led to new levels of intimacy with God. Mother Teresa once famously said, "You never know Jesus is all you need, until Jesus is all you have." When things start getting stripped away from us, we discover God is enough and we pursue Him with greater vigor. We go after the one true source of satisfying, replenishing love. He is the fountain of life. The Living Water. The Bread of Life. He alone can satisfy. So, one of the ways that God can redeem this current hardship in our lives is if we use it to lean into Him and draw near.

James 4:8 instructs us, "Come near to God and he will come near to you." The prophet

Jeremiah once said to a people in exile, "You will seek me and find me when you seek me with all your heart. I will be found by you" (Jeremiah 29:13-14).

When I was about thirty, on one of the darkest days of my young life, where my heart was broken beyond what I had ever experienced to that point in my young life, I turned to the Psalms to seek God. The Psalms are a prayer book. They are the cries of people who have gone before us on this spiritual journey and they have experienced all the hurts and pains of life that we have experienced. And they process their pain and they cry out to God in the Psalms. They have often been so helpful to me in times of hardship and heartache. On this particular occasion I was up late alone with God with my broken heart. And I came across Psalm 34:18, "The Lord is close to the brokenhearted and saves those who are crushed in spirit." I sobbed when I read it and I felt the presence of God flood into my pain. I lived there in that verse over the coming months and I claimed the promise as my own. I pursed God with unrelenting fervor. I discovered God in those days in ways that I could never have discovered Him without that heartache.

Each of us has to develop our own history with God. One of the ways we develop history with God is in the hardship of life. If we process hardship carefully, we find God in our pain.

Access

I have often said the one thing God most wants is access. He wants access to our hearts and souls; He wants access to our inner beings. But sometimes our heart grows hardened in places like soil that can no longer receive the seeds sown by the farmer. When the soil of our heart grows hard, it needs to be pierced to give Him access, just like the earthly soil – the farmer has to turn it over so it can receive the seed. *Hardship pierces the heart and makes us accessible to God in places that were once inaccessible.* We have to do our part – our part is to draw near. Our part is to cooperate with his redeeming work and give Him the access that He seeks.

If we are going to draw near to God, this means that we cannot take offense at the hardship that has entered our life. Often in hardship, we take offense at God. Remember John the Baptist? John was the one who recognized Jesus when Mary came to visit Elizabeth and John was still in his Mother's womb (Luke 1:41)! He leaped in her womb because he knew Jesus. John was the one who spotted Jesus walking along and cried out, "Behold, the Lamb of God who takes away the sin of the world!" (John 1:29). But when John faced his cruel and imminent death, he doubted. He questioned. He sent his followers to Jesus with a message to ask Jesus, "Are you the one?" John knew his whole life that Jesus was the one. But hardship weakens our grip on truth; it makes us question what we once knew with certainty. It diminishes our perception of the goodness of God at the center of our souls.

Jesus tells John's disciples, "Go back and report to John what you hear and see: The blind receive sight, the lame walk, those who have leprosy are cleansed, the deaf hear, the dead are raised, and the good news is proclaimed to the poor. Blessed is anyone who does not stumble on account of me." Literally, blessed is anyone who does not take offense on account of me. Look at the evidence. Look at what Jesus has done. Look at the Scripture. Look at the cross. Look at His miracles. Look at your life. Look at what He has done. Reflect on the goodness of God and hold on to the truth without taking offense.

I developed a motto for seeking God that has guided and helped me over the years. This is my motto: Ever grateful, never satisfied, relentlessly pursuing God for more of Himself, never taking offense. I had to add the section about never taking offense because I found myself in John's shoes too often. I was passionately pursuing God with great expectations and too often I found myself hurt and disappointed that God didn't come through the way I wanted or expected Him to. I had to make a covenant with God that I would never take offense again. It was blocking my path to deeper places with my Savior. I do not always understand why God does what He does, or why God allows what He allows, or why God answers the way He does, but I know I can trust Him because of the cross. I know He is with me and He is for me. He has proven it by his life and death on the cross. I decided I would embrace the discomforts of life without letting it diminish my perception of the goodness of God. I determined I would trust Him without offense.

Seasons like this can challenge my commitment not to take offense at God. As an author, I have spent the past few years building up my platform for my books to sell. It's not easy. But I made steady progress and this year I was selling 350 *Soul Care* books a week through Amazon and bookstores. But six weeks after COVID-19 hit, and all of the bookstores closed, I was distributing just 40 books per week. Years of building torn down in a moment. It is the second time in my life I have spent years building something only to watch it torn down. It is a grievous thing for a person like me to experience. But, I have determined that I will not take offense at God. So, I grieved it. I felt the loss and the sadness. I expressed my heartache and pain. Then I surrendered it. It took me several days to process it, but I have determined that I will not take offense at God, because it hardens my heart and disrupts my intimacy with Him. I have some very clear promises about those books that I have written that have not been fulfilled. If I am going to continue to trust in the goodness of God for my future, I must grieve the hurts of my present and my past so that my heart doesn't grow hard.

I have a long track record with God and His goodness. He has proven Himself to me over and over. I am not going to take offense in the present and require He proves Himself to me again. I have had friends over the years who said things to me like, "I need to spend time with you to make sure I see your heart so I can trust you." In the beginning that was ok, because we were getting to know each other. But after a while it is hurtful because I have been with them long enough that I have a track record of loyalty established with them and I expect them to go to the bank of our previous interactions and give me the benefit of the doubt. Trust me. I am for you. We talked it through, and they agreed to give me the benefit of the doubt in future encounters. Their trust deepened our relationship. I am admittedly weak and imperfect; I fail and let people down. I sin and have to ask for forgiveness. *Jesus is unrelenting beauty, untarnished goodness, unstoppable grace, unending love, and unflappable peace. He never errs, never sins, never has impure motives. He has an eternally trustworthy track record.* You can trust Him without taking offense even in the darkest seasons of life.

Let me give you a couple of practical thoughts for drawing near to God in this season of chaos. They have helped me over the years, and I pray that they will help you in this current crisis.

Alone with God

First, get alone with God often in these dark days. In Psalm 11, David who was well acquainted with crises, asked a pertinent question: "When the foundations are being destroyed, what can the righteous do?" Great question. As I watch our world hole up in isolation in fear of a disease that is ravaging our planet and with the increasing dread of the economic realities that it is leaving in its wake, it sure feels like an appropriate question for us to ask in our time. At the time that I write this, over thirty three million people have filed for unemployment in the US – it is a record shattering number of jobless people. We've watched the stock market plummet from its all-time high point; it has rebounded some, but not to where it was. We sit by fearful and uncertain about when things will return to normal.

David answered his own question in the next verse, "The Lord is in his holy temple; the Lord is on his heavenly throne" (Psalm 11:4). David's answer to his current crisis was that God was still on His throne. Today, in our crisis God is still on His throne and He has no challengers for His throne. We are seated with Christ in the heavenly realms (Eph 2). We are citizens of heaven (Phil 3). We are secure in His eternal grip. We surely cannot make sense of it all, but we can surely hold on to His goodness while He holds on to us. When it feels like the world is falling apart, I need to get this image clear in my heart: God is still on His throne. He isn't nervous. He isn't apathetic. He isn't impotent. He sees. He cares. He understands. He redeems all things.

The Psalms are so helpful for me to voice my heart to God in these uncertain times. Psalm 116 is another beautiful Psalm. David has escaped the throes of death and he is expressing his gratitude. He makes a striking comment in v.7, "Return, O my soul, to your rest; for the Lord has dealt bountifully with you" (ESV). I love that verse. *As long as I can maintain my grip on the goodness of God, peace and rest can maintain its grip on me.* I lose my rest when I stop believing God has enough bountiful goodness to deal with my current reality. When the fright of my current reality overtakes my grip on God's bountiful goodness, I lose my rest; my peace is shattered. If I believe God is bountifully good and has enough resources to provide for me in an economic crisis, I can maintain my peace even when the foundations of our economic world are shaken to the core. But when I stop believing in the bountiful goodness, the abundance of God, then my rest will be robbed, and my peace will be purloined.

Every day I start the day alone with God. I usually mediate on some Scripture that reminds me of who God is, what God is like, and I reignite my faith. I pray the things that are on my heart; I talk to God about my concerns, my fears, my problems, my heartaches, my needs, my finances, my loved ones, the world's crisis, and all the things that are preoccupying my attention. I consciously seek to shift my heart out of the fear zone into the faith zone, out of self-focus into God-focus, out of independence and into dependence on God.

Jesus told us to pray, "Give us this day our daily bread." When we come from the land of plenty, we often don't have to exercise daily dependence for our basic necessities. Our cupboards are full, our bank accounts have some cushion, our supplies are our insurance, our resources are our comfort. But when the foundations are being destroyed, we learn to lean into God with a newfound daily dependence and we discover God in new intimacies. It isn't fun but it is beautiful. We come to the stark realization that we can control so little and God is truly our source.

Quite often at the end of the day I have to come back to God and spend time with God again. I pray some Psalms and re-center my focus on Him before I go to bed. He is still on His throne regardless of what bad things may have happened during the day. He still isn't nervous. I can still depend on Him because He is trustworthy. I must constantly renew my focus on His trustworthiness if I am going to draw near to God. I cannot draw near to One that I do not trust.

As you spend time with God and strengthen your wobbly faith, it is necessary to factor in eternity. David did this in Psalm 116. Psalm 116:15, David writes, "Precious in the sight of the Lord is the death of those faithful to him." It is an interesting line because David has just been rescued from the throes of death. So, why does he say this? Because some day death will come calling for him and for us. He rejoiced in his temporary reprieve from death on this occasion, but it was only a matter of time before death got the upper hand. One day death would come calling and he wouldn't walk away from its deadly snare. *Our ultimate security isn't in our temporary victories, but in God's eternal Home*. This is why we can rest – no matter what. At this crucial time, sink deep roots in your eternal Home and your loving Heavenly Father who sits upon His throne unchallenged. There may be temporary setbacks, evil may have its way at times in frightful force, but God will always have the last word and evil will be vanquished once and for all in heaven. God's power will often be manifest in our temporal circumstances, His faithfulness will be visible to those who look for it, and His victories will surely be rendered in the end of time.

Grieving

Second, if we are going to draw near to God, we have to take time to grieve in this season. COVID-19 is not just a killer it is a thief. It is robbing us of many of our freedoms, pleasures and comforts. And we need to grieve the losses we are experiencing in order to maintain a healthy soul. The Psalms, once again, are very useful to help us give voice to our grief. A large percentage of the Psalms are lament Psalms; the Psalmist is in a time of crisis and he is crying out to God. He is processing his fears, his pain, his loss, his grief, and all of his messy emotions. He is raw but reverent, honest but honorable. This is critically important for drawing near to God.

If we don't process our grief, our trust will be diminished. We can't whitewash pain and heartache with pithy religious phrases or a memorized verse from the Bible. This is what a religious person does – they take a truth and put it on like an outer garment, but they fail to internalize it in their inner being so that it becomes part of their life. They have the right words, but religion is skin-deep. *Religious people often fail to internalize eternal truths and they face life with a thin soul. True trust is developed when hardships are authentically processed and the pain-stricken heart comes to restful surrender in the eternal arms of the Man of Sorrows.* Though we don't always understand, yet we trust Him because He is the One who entered our pain and suffered with us and suffered for us on the cross.

When we are going through the darkest of times and we are processing our grief, it often feels like we are losing our grip on faith. It doesn't feel like God draws near to the broken-hearted when we are in a season of grieving. The Psalmists acknowledge this human condition. This morning I was processing the sadness that was in my heart due to the losses of this season. It is my 55th birthday today as I write, on April 10, 2020. I turned to the Psalms as I so often do to process my emotions. This has been my practice for 30 years. I turn to the Psalm of the day of the week. So, today is April 10th, I turned and opened Psalm 10. Then I add 30 and pray the Psalms that resonate with me most. Psalm 10, 40, 70, 100, 130 were the Psalms today. (Some people on the 29th do Psalm 29, 59, 89, and 149, saving Psalm 119 for the 31st of every month – since it is the longest Psalm). Psalm 10:1 starts with, "Why, Lord, do you stand far off? Why do you hide yourself in times of trouble?" I have felt that before too. I have been feeling it a little this week. I have found myself carrying some sadness quite often in this season. The Psalm gave voice to my heart.

In the lament Psalms, the Psalmists process their grief openly, but they always end in trust and surrender. They wrestle with God; they process deep emotion and they ask hard questions, but they always look up and out of their pain by the end of the Psalm. They turn to God in surrendered trust. Sometimes we fail to get out of sadness, because we do not look up and out of our sadness with trust and surrender to God. The Psalmists lead us through to that place.

This morning, I grieved over the losses of this season. They are real, hard, and painful. In some ways, I feel like I did when I saw hundreds of people leave the church that I planted. It felt like I had spent a lifetime building this church that I loved, only to watch so many people walk away. It was draining, discouraging, disappointing and disheartening. I feel that again in this season as I feel a tremendous loss in momentum in the Kingdom work that I was called to and engaged in. So, I grieved. I let tears flow. Then I surrendered – I gave myself to the One with nail prints in His hands. He is trustworthy.

The grief is real, but temporal. His goodness is sure, and eternal. The loss is hard, but impermanent. The gains of heaven are beautiful, and everlasting. Grieving helps me to get out what is inside and is threatening my perception of God's goodness. And grieving rejuvenates my perspective on eternity. I let go of the temporal and I hold on to the eternal. Grieving also helps me to die to self. Some of the reason I feel pain and loss in this season is connected to my self-life. I want my comforts, I want my opportunities, I want my position, I want my life like it is. But that is too much about me and what I want, so when I grieve I get to the place where I can let go of what I have lost and die to my desires and wants and bring myself into alignment with God's will, and God's ways. The fact that I need to die to self, doesn't invalidate the reality that I need to grieve. I grieve and I die to self. I let go of desires and I surrender. This is part of the process of Christ being formed in me.

Giving Thanks

Third, if we are going to draw near to God, we need to take time to give thanks in the seasons of darkness. Paul said, "Rejoice always, pray continually, give thanks in all circumstances; for this is God's will for you in Christ Jesus" (1 Thessalonians 5:16-18). *There are only two times to give thanks – when you feel like it and when you don't. And the time you most need to exercise thanksgiving is precisely when you don't feel like it.* Thanksgiving is a gateway to the presence of God. Psalm 100, another of the Psalms I prayed this morning, says "Enter his gates with thanksgiving and his courts with praise; give thanks to him and praise his name" (Psalm 100:4). It is an act of deep trust and dependence to thank God in the darkest hours. *Thanksgiving is a mood changer, an atmosphere shifter, a light bearer, a despair breaker, a hope dealer.* Thanksgiving is an opportunity to display our trust even when the foundations are crumbling, because our trust isn't in the foundation, but in God Himself. Anyone can give thanks when the cupboards are full, the bank account is plush, and the circumstances are fruitful. But to give thanks in times of lack is an honorable and noble act of faith that brings pleasure to the heart of God.

You will never get to give God thanks in difficult times in heaven because there won't be difficult times in heaven. Here on earth is your only opportunity to display the kind of faith that can thank God, worship God, and trust God in the darkest hour. In heaven, there will not be any darkness, so trusting God will be easy. But on earth it is hard, it is a choice, it is an act of faith based on the Word of God, based on the character of God, based on God's proven track record, not based on the circumstances of life. It is an intentional decision to trust the eternal promises of God are more lasting and real than our fleeting temporal problems. *Life is life. God is God. Life is sometimes harsh and cruel and difficult. But life does not change the character of God. God is still God and God is still good.* And you can still trust Him, and you can still give Him thanks.

In one of my darkest seasons in life I called upon my friend, Ron Walborn. I was in deep grief and it felt like I was losing my grip on the goodness of God. Ron listened. He grieved with me. And then he said something that changed my life. He said, "Bud, you are an intense guy. You need to have more fun." It didn't seem like very spiritual advice. But I took on fun as a spiritual discipline. I decided I would be as intentional about having fun as I was about reading my Bible and praying. I started to engage in regular fun activities with a thankful heart. James reminds us that every good gift comes from our Father above (James 1:17). I participated in fun activities with a grateful heart as a regular spiritual discipline. It produced an unexpected and remarkable result. It restored the goodness of God to the center of my being. Hardship has a way of loosening our grip on the goodness of God at the center of our souls; participating in fun with gratitude restores our perception of the goodness of God. Psalm 34:8 says, "Taste and see that the Lord is good." But how do you taste and see that the Lord is good? You can't lick Him. One of the ways that we taste and see that God is good is by participating in God's good gifts with a grateful heart.

So, in this season of prolonged world agony take time to remember the goodness of God. Take time to have fun with gratitude. Take long slow walks in nature and take a deep breath and feel the goodness of God in creation. Watch funny movies with your family or a friend, even if it is at a distance and laugh together. Tell old stories of God's faithfulness, and humorous anecdotes of days gone by and revel in the goodness of God. Talk to good friends over the phone and recall good times and smile. It will be good for your soul.

Silence and Stillness

Fourth, to draw near to God in the midst of a crisis I have found that it is particularly helpful to sit with God in silence and stillness. Psalm 46:10 says, "Be still and know that I am God." But the context is a time of trouble, v.1, "God is our refuge and strength, an ever-present help in trouble." When we are afraid, we get an adrenaline boost in our bodies and it speeds everything up inside. Our mind races, our heart speeds up, our reflex reaction is often to act impulsively. But the Psalmist does exactly the opposite of what his body is dictating. He slows everything down and gets still before the Lord. He focuses on God's ever loving, ever faithful, ever capable presence. In the stillness, he draws strength.

So, when I spend time alone with God, inevitably I end up in silence. Psalm 62:1, "For God alone my soul waits in silence; from Him comes my salvation." *Once you have prayed everything that you can pray, said everything you can say and done everything you can do, all that is left is to wait upon the Lord in silence.* Often, we are tempted to pray in fear, and it is a feeble attempt to try to control the outcomes of our life. Give up control and rest in His arms. Sitting with God in silence is an act of giving up control; it is an act of surrendered trust and dependence. I think this is what David was doing in Psalm 11. He remembers God is in His holy temple; He is seated on His heavenly throne. And he comes to God in trustful resting dependence. This is what the Psalmist is doing here in Psalm 46 and again in Psalm 62. This is a common spiritual practice by those who have gone through crisis for generations before us.

Let me give you some practical tips on preparing your heart to spend time in silence with God. Often when we go to spend time in silence our minds are busy and racing and we can't get still and quiet internally before the Lord. So, what do we do to prepare ourselves to meet with God in silence?

To prepare myself for silence I always start by praying through my agenda for the day. I literally pray through my to do list and my agenda. I do this because otherwise these things are going to preoccupy my mind when I go to be quiet. I am off-loading my distractions. I then make sure my confessions are current. I let the Lord search me to see if there is anything I need to confess that could block my connection to Him. Psalm 139:23-24 says, "Search me, God, and know my heart; test me and know my anxious thoughts. See if there is any offensive way in me and lead me in the way everlasting." After I confess, I pray through the fearful things – the anxious thoughts. Let the Holy Spirit show you any barriers to His presence. Deal with those before the Lord. Next I take some time to meditate on Scripture or worship or both. I am now ready to move closer, to draw near with some of these disciplines. I want to give God my full attention and enter His presence. Now I am ready to be still.

I live on a lake. Often when I get up in the morning the lake is perfectly still and if someone was on the other side of the lake, they could speak to me and I could hear them. But if it was a day like today, where the wind is howling and the lake is choppy, that person could yell, and I couldn't make out a word they were saying. Our soul is like that lake. We have to do what we can to cultivate an inner stillness before we are ready to move into God's presence with a peaceful quiet mind.

In quietness before the Lord, all I am attempting to do is to fix my loving attention on God's presence. I just want to be with Him. In his presence there is peace; in his presence there is strength; in his presence there is comfort. Draw near in silence. Be still and know that He is God.

Pursue His Face

Lastly, to draw near in this time of crisis we must not neglect to pursue His presence. Sometimes in a season of hardship we can pursue God passionately for answers to our prayers and solutions to our problems. We are desperate, so we seek God for breakthroughs, for miracles, for protection, for provision and for practical help. God is a good Father and He wants us to come with all of our requests and needs. But at some point, if we are really going to draw near to Him, we have to make a shift and pursue Him merely for Himself. David prays in Psalm 16, "I say to the Lord, 'You are my Lord; I have no good apart from you.' . . . The Lord is my chosen portion and my cup; you hold my lot. The lines have fallen for me in pleasant places; indeed, I have a beautiful inheritance. . . In your presence there is fullness of joy" (Psalm 16:2,5-6,11, ESV). David is pursuing God in a time of crisis; death is near, and David pursues God for protection, for deliverance. But his ultimate pursuit is for God's presence.

It is God's presence that is David's chosen portion. He has no good apart from the presence of God. It is the Lord Himself that David needs, more than deliverance, more than answered prayer. The Lord is David's beautiful inheritance. Even if he dies, the Lord is still his inheritance because God is eternal, and God has the final word. In the presence of God, even in the midst of crisis, even in the midst of real and imminent danger, there is the fullness of joy.

There is a famous line in Nehemiah 8 that people quote a lot, v.10, "The joy of the Lord is our strength." But most of the time people quote it, they don't really understand it. The people of God had rebelled; they had actually wandered so far from God they had misplaced the book of the Law. When the Law was found and read to the people, they wept since they realized how far they had wandered from God, how deeply they had grieved His heart. But Nehemiah stood before the people and said, "This day is holy to our Lord. Do not grieve, for the joy of the Lord is your strength." The Lord was joyous because His people had come home; they had repented. Their hearts had melted, and they were contrite; their hearts once again welcomed the presence of God. And God was deeply moved. It gave God great joy that His people had returned, that they were back into right relationship with Him; this was what He longed for, this was what He wanted most. They wanted Him and He wanted them. When the people of God choose God over sin, when they choose God over stuff, when they choose God over their idols, when they choose God once again as their heart's desire and primary affection, God feels great joy. It is God's joy in our return that is our strength. When we repent, we feel the joy of the Lord because we are drawing near and His joyful presence over our return strengths our inner beings.

This is the fullness of joy that David discovered in God's presence. David longed for God, not just for his deliverance, but for God Himself. And God was pleased, delighted with David's heart, delighted with David's companionship. As David pursued God, he felt God's joy over him and his heart was satisfied.

In this season, don't just pursue God's hand for deliverance. Yes. Pursue Him for help – He is a good Father who answers His children's prayers. But don't just seek His hands, seek His face. Pursue His presence. He is our inheritance, not His gifts, not His deliverance. In His presence is the fullness of joy.

It was actually pursuing God's presence that lead me into the practice of silence. I was seeking His face, not His hands, and I realized very quickly that words couldn't get me there. So, I began to sit in silence just attending to His loving presence. In the silence, I found His loving presence and His face. Worship has also been a key pathway for me to discover God's face. For me personally, the most helpful thing I've done in worship is just soaking. I let worship music play that moves my heart and again I fix my attention on His presence. Meditation on Scripture has been another key path for me to find God's face. I read some Scripture slowly and I linger with a phrase or a word or sentence when the Spirit highlights it to my heart. Often, I can feel the Spirit stirring within me as I read a particular verse and I will linger there with that verse. The presence of God is there with me, speaking to me, in that moment; He is revealing Himself to me.

These are some key paths to seek His face that have helped me. Find your path. Pursue his presence. Seek His face. Apart from Him, you have no good thing. He is the One you need. Take time and draw near.

Chapter 4: God Redeems

As I said earlier, show me how a person handles a crisis and it will tell me a lot about the person's interior life. Crises reveal the cracks in the inner walls of our soul. These difficult seasons expose us to the things in our interior life that are out of alignment with God. They reveal undealt with issues. Hardships expose our dysfunctions and sins. They uncover false beliefs that are like faulty foundations in our soul. They trigger unprocessed wounding to resurface in fresh anxiety. They shine light into the unhealed regions of our souls that need God's care and repair. They uncover the weak spots in the walls of our soul. So, crises become crucial opportunities for life change. It is often our darkest seasons of life that produce the greatest transformation.

It was that marriage crisis that allowed me to discover the principles that I write about in my book *Soul Care* and become a healthier person which eventually led to a healthier marriage. During that crisis I was alone with God one day and He said to me, "I want you to give me thanks for this marriage pain." I said, "Lord, even in the midst of this hardship, I am grateful for many things, but the marriage pain is not one of them." I sensed the Spirit whispering to me, "One day you will be more grateful for this marriage crisis than almost anything other experience in your life. I want you to give me thanks in faith today before you see that come to pass." So, I did. I gave God thanks for something I could not see my way out of, but of course, now I see. Once you have already experienced God's redeeming hand at work in a crisis, it doesn't take faith to look back on it and see how God could use it. But when you are standing in the midst of a present crisis and looking into an unknown future it takes great faith to trust God to redeem this current hardship. If I had waited to give God thanks after God delivered me that would not have required trust on my part at all.

That crisis taught me key *Soul Care* principles that changed my life and ended up helping thousands of others. Jen and I are going to celebrate our 30th anniversary in June. We are in the best years of our life together, but that wouldn't be true unless I went through that crisis and learned those principles. That crisis was critical for my transformation on the spiritual journey and allowed me to draw near to God like never before.

I went through a ministry crisis where many people left the church and many people attacked me. Again, I was alone with God in the midst of that crisis and I sought the Lord at the monastery. I said, "Lord, why? I don't understand why these things are happening. I am just sincerely trying to do what you have asked me to do." The Lord said, "I'm answering your prayer." That made me pause. I said, "Lord, I don't know what I've been praying, but I promise, if you tell me – I'll stop!" He said, "For over a decade you have been praying, 'Lord, give me the ability to impart your Spirit like the Apostles for the sake of advancing your Kingdom.' This is what it takes. I'm answering your prayer." I said, "Then answer my prayer." And He did. That season prepared me to enter into a season where the Lord started moving in new waves of significant power. I couldn't have gotten to that new season without the crisis.

God is a Master at redeeming evil and making good from it. Romans 8:28f, Paul said, "And we know that in all things God works for the good of those who love him, who have been called according to his purpose. For those God foreknew he also predestined to be conformed to the image of his Son, that he might be the firstborn among many brothers and sisters. And those he predestined, he also called; those he called, he also justified; those he justified, he also glorified."

Paul is not saying that everything that comes into our lives is good. There are plenty of evil things that happen in this fallen world. God does not ordain evil; God redeems evil. Some people have been raped – that is not ordained by God. But God is so good that when He comes and touches some evil thing done against you, He can make good out of it in your life.

I think God can redeem all of the evil things in the world and make good come out of it – whether it is a personal crisis or a corporate crisis like the one we are going through together now. And in this case, the corporate crisis is going to create many personal crises as well. Just consider again that over thirty-three million people having filed for unemployment in the first seven weeks of our social isolation in the US. That is going to create long lasting consequences for many families. A local family owned restaurant that has been in business for over twenty years closed its doors this week because of this issue. I was talking with another business owner who has been in business for over thirty years and when I asked him how they were weathering the storm he responded, "I hope we can make it." He owns one of the busiest restaurants I know in our area and he simply hopes they can make it at this point. The corporate crisis is creating many personal crises in its wake. But God can redeem them all in our nations, and in our personal lives.

Our Strength and Our Shield

David often found himself in crises and he called out to the Lord in those dark places. Over and over again the Lord delivered him. In Psalm 28:7, David said, "The Lord is my strength and my shield; my heart trusts in him, and he helps me. My heart leaps for joy, and with my song I praise him." Sometimes the Lord is our shield - God shields us from what crisis that comes or way – He protects us; He spares us from the crises or its effects. Like David, our hearts are full of joy and we praise Him for his mighty help. He has delivered my family from cancer, from financial disasters with miraculous provisions, and from painful circumstances with supernatural interventions.

Sometimes the Lord is our strength. There are times when the Lord does not shield us from the hardship, He gives us the strength to go through it. We have to experience the suffering, but He is with us; He is present. He gives us the inner strength we need to see us through and to come out the other side victorious. We pray, like the other times when God delivers us from it, but the crisis comes. We ask God to take it away, but the crisis remains. His strength is present; his presence is strength. He is there with us and for us. Often these are places that we would not choose to go on our own, but we could not be the people we have become today without going through these difficulties with God. It is often in these dark valleys that we discover the strength of God we didn't even know was available to us.

Corrie Ten Boom was a Christian woman who endured the Nazi concentration camps because she and her family helped Jewish people. When she was a little girl she went to her father and said, "Daddy, I'm afraid I'll never be strong enough to be a martyr for Jesus Christ." "Tell me," father said, "when you take a train trip from Harlem to Amsterdam when do I give you the money for the ticket? Three weeks before?" "No, Daddy, you give me the money for the ticket just before we get on the train." "That is right," her father said, "And so it is with God's strength. Our wise Father in heaven knows when you are going to need things too. Today you do not need the strength to be a martyr, but as soon as you're called upon to be a martyr for Jesus, He will supply the strength you need just in time." (*Tramp for the Lord*, p.117-118)

Your Father might deliver you from this crisis in your life. It maybe you are shielded from sickness and financial hardship. But it is possible that your Father will not shield you; He will just give you the strength to see you through. He will supply the strength you need just in time. You may have to endure the sickness; you may have to suffer the loss of loved ones from it. You may even suffer financial hardship, or unemployment. You may have to endure some of the impact of this hardship and yet you will discover that his strong presence is enough. His strength can see you through all the way to eternity.

Later on, in Corrie Ten Boom's life she did indeed have to suffer persecution at the hand of the Nazi's. Her father and sister died in the concentration camp. They remained faithful to Jesus to the end and now are with Him in heaven and have received their reward. Corrie found that her Father gave her strength to get through. I have read thousands of books in my lifetime. Corrie is one of my favorite authors. Her book, *Tramp for the Lord*, is one of my all-time favorite books. She is a beautiful soul with profound depth because she discovered the strength of God that sustained her and shaped her in the darkest hour. God saw her through. He redeemed her suffering and she traveled the world telling the story of God's redeeming love. Hundreds of thousands of people were impacted for eternity because of what she suffered and the worldwide platform it gave her. The fact is that Corrie Ten Boom only became the powerful woman of God she was because God saw her through the suffering. If God had spared her from all of it, she likely never would have written and I would not have been impacted by her life.

As a parent there are many things I would like to protect my children from experiencing. But if I stepped in and protected them, it could keep them from maturing. There were times in my formative years I experienced rejection and heartache. My parents may have wanted to protect me from those things. But those rejections formed my heart; one of them was the very thing I that turned my heart to God. My Father did not shield me from them, but He did strengthen me in them.

Pain Reveals

One of the great things about pain is that it reveals broken places within us and opens our hearts to the need for change. You may discover in this hardship that you are feeling anxiety at levels you have not experienced before. You may find yourself becoming irritable and angry. You may start to slide into depression or have to grapple with sadness. You may feel high levels of stress. You may discover that you are starting to experience tension in your marriage. It seemed like before the crisis you were doing fine, but now confined in isolation together you are starting to experience new levels of conflict. There is nothing like a crisis to reveal the broken places in our interior life. Give God access to these places; process them with Him. This is a season of redemption. This is an opportune time for life change.

Perhaps you are discovering that your worldly attachments and comforts were actually a source of strength for you that were keeping you from depending on God in ways that you didn't even know. But now it is exposed through fear, anxiety and worry. Don't run from it; turn to God. Die to what you need to die to, detach from what you need to detach from, surrender what you need to surrender. Feel the weakness that is apparent in the temporary attachments and draw from the eternal strength of God's loving presence. It could be an opportunity like no other for you to draw near to God and develop spiritual depth.

Paul had a crisis, what he called "a thorn in the flesh," that he asked the Lord to deliver him from, but the Lord did not deliver him. Rather the Lord said to Paul, "My grace is sufficient for you, for my power is made perfect in weakness" (2 Corinthians 12:9). Sometimes God does not deliver us from a crisis, but He does strengthen us in it. We cannot discover God's strength and power without our weaknesses being exposed. Our weakness is God's opportunity to display his strength.

Maybe you are one of the millions of people who lost their job in this current crisis or you like many others that I know have taken a cut in pay. It isn't uncommon for people to lose their job and discover they were gaining some sense of significance and security from their position and their title. And when that position is gone, it feels like the foundation beneath their feet is crumbling. The inner life begins to rattle and manifests in unhealthy emotional reactions. Take advantage of this opportunity to get on the secure foundation of your identity in Christ. Do the deep work of the soul in this season.

If you are starting to feel some of the symptomatic expressions of the cracks in your soul, take time to get alone with God and seek Him for wisdom. One of the key questions that I ask in my book *Soul Care* is: "What's underneath that?" What is driving that symptom? Process the emotions that you feel. Process the fear, the anxiety, the grief, the loss, the pain. Journaling is a great tool to help you process. Write it down, express your emotions. Get them out before the Lord. But don't stop there. Ask the Lord this key *Soul Care* question. I journal, I reflect, I pray, I ask God for wisdom and I talk to others about these matters as well. Sometimes someone else can lend me a perspective that gives me the insight I need. Get to the roots; don't just deal with the fruits.

We have to learn how to wrestle with God. We need to take time alone with God in these seasons of crisis and wrestle with God until we find breakthrough. In our marriage crisis I started by praying about the symptoms. They were "God fix it" prayers. Fix Jen. Fix our marriage. Fix the conflict. But those prayers are surface prayers. They don't go deep enough. For God to fix the crisis in our marriage, He had to fix the issues in our soul that were out of alignment with Him. The marriage crisis was merely symptomatic of deeper soul issues. I had hurt that I needed to be healed; I had anger and I needed to forgive. I had lies that I believed about my identity that I needed to replace with the truth. I had fears that I didn't even know were inside my heart that I needed to drive out with the perfect love of God. That marriage crisis was a gift that led me to deep breakthroughs. I couldn't have gotten there without the crisis. The crisis created the crucible for change.

If you are starting to see some of the cracks in your soul in this season of world crisis, why don't you take the time to work through *Soul Care*. Don't just read it. Really work through it. Process deeply. Wrestle with God. Work through it with some other people. Let God redeem the crisis in your life. It could make all the difference.

Gateway to Life Change

Crises are often the gateway to life change. There are many things in my life that I never would have chosen to go through but couldn't have grown up without. I wrote *Soul Care* to help people process these broken places in their interior life so that they could experience the freedom and fullness that Jesus has won for them on the cross. *Soul Care* isn't really a book to be read; it covers key principles of freedom that need to be lived. Only when we work through these areas and integrate these principles into the core of our inner being can we live free. The Western world has focused on knowledge-based discipleship; we have assumed that if people just knew the right things, they would do the right things. But knowledge without integration cannot lead to transformation. Since this crisis began, I have had many people write to me and say, "I am so grateful I worked through *Soul Care* before this Coronavirus crisis. I couldn't have handled it without having done the inner work." If you haven't done that work yet, now is a great time.

In prosperous, comfort-based societies it is hard not to rely on our own capabilities and resources. It is hard not to become attached to the temporary, and it is virtually impossible for the temporary attachments not to tarnish our affections for Jesus. I have felt the financial fear and loss of this season in my own life, but I have given my life to fight for revival. And as hard as financial loss is, I would rather lose everything and see revival come, then hold on to my temporary comforts and miss a critical Kingdom moment in history. This is a redemptive moment, an opportune time for us to do a deep inner work of consecrating ourselves to God. Take advantage of this isolation to pursue Jesus and give yourself wholeheartedly to Him.

It is also possible for God to use a crisis like this to detach us from our material resources as a source of comfort and security, not so that He can remove them from us, but so that He can restore them to us with new redemptive purpose. If we detach from the temporal, and sink deep roots in the eternal, it is quite possible that the resources we once held on to for security and comfort will now be released for Kingdom purposes. The shift in mentality could be the very thing God needs to bring about new Kingdom advancement. *Detachment doesn't always mean the removal of our possessions from our hands; it means the removal of our possessions from our hearts.*

This is a time to re-examine our hearts and lives and give ourselves fully and unreservedly to Jesus. There is no peace without surrender. We must yield ourselves to the Lordship of Christ in fresh ways in times of crises. When I was a young man it was the crisis of a broken heart that caused me to take stock of my life and turn wholeheartedly to Jesus. Prior to that moment in my life, I had gone to church. I read my Bible through every year. I prayed. I served at my local church. But Jesus was still not at the center of my life. He was there; He was involved. But he was peripheral. That breakup changed me because it exposed that I wasn't really following Jesus with all my heart. Jesus was an add-on to my life, not the center of my life. Bonhoeffer once famously said in his book *The Cost of Discipleship*, "When Christ calls a man, He bids him come and die." Jesus said, "Whoever wants to be my disciple must deny themselves and take up their cross daily and follow me. For whoever wants to save their life will lose it, but whoever loses their life for me will save it" (Luke 9:23-24). He later said, "If anyone comes to me and does not hate father and mother, wife and children, brothers and sisters – yes, even life itself – such a person cannot be my disciple. And whoever does not carry their cross and follow me cannot be my disciple" (Luke 14:26-27).

Listen, Jesus doesn't hate your Mom. That's not his point. His point is that He has to have the number one place in your heart. He has to be your primary loyalty. Discipleship, following

Jesus, is really about changing cultures. You are moving from the culture of your family of origin, and people of origin, and nation of origin, to the culture of the King and his Kingdom. When Kingdom culture clashes with your American culture, or your Asian culture, or your Canadian culture, or your family of origin culture, if you don't choose Kingdom culture, you're not a follower. Not in that area you're not. You have a prior loyalty, a deeper loyalty, and Jesus is not your King. Times like this expose our deeper priorities and superior loyalties. That's just what crises do. And times like this are moments in our personal history with God to surrender all, to bring all of our life, all of our hearts, all of our actions under the loyalty of the King and his Kingdom.

God wants to redeem this crisis to allow in all of our lives so that we come more fully into alignment with Him. That is where freedom and fullness is found – when we are in alignment with Jesus. When we are out of alignment the cracks of our soul start to appear and create symptomatic expressions of sin and dysfunction in our lives.

Some of you have been to church your whole life, but Jesus has not had the center of your heart. He has not been enthroned in your heart above all other priorities and all other loyalties. And now is the time. Now is the time to go all in, to surrender, to put Him first, to center your life around Him. So many years ago, when I was a freshman in college and I suffered that broken heart, what that crisis revealed was that my heart was not loyal to the King above all else. And I surrendered that day. I simply prayed, "From now on, you lead, and I'll follow. You've got me. I'm yours." And I meant it. From that day forth I sought to put Jesus first – I have not always done it well; I have sinned too many times to remember since then, but from that day forth, it has been my sincere and unwavering desire to follow Jesus wholeheartedly, though I am deeply flawed and sinful. Every other day has been working out that decision to surrender everything to Jesus. Start there. Consecrate your life to Christ for He bids you come and die. It is only in death to self that we can truly live.

Redeeming the Crisis Corporately

God cannot only redeem this time in our lives individually, but He can redeem this crisis in our lives corporately – as the church, and even in the world. Think about the persecution that took place in Acts. The Spirit was poured out on the day of Pentecost. The church was launched with supernatural power. Thousands were being converted, lives were being changed, people were being healed, the power of the Risen Christ was on display. And then the religious leaders tried to put a stop to this new wildfire that broke out. They decided to persecute the church and the church scattered as the persecution broke out. The people had gathered in Jerusalem for the feast of Pentecost and when the Spirit was poured out, they didn't want to leave. It was too good to depart. But when people started suffering and dying in Jerusalem for the name of Jesus, people fled Jerusalem and they went back to their towns and homes and businesses around the Roman Empire. Acts 8:1, "On that day a great persecution broke out against the church in Jerusalem, and all except the apostles were scattered throughout Judea and Samaria. . . Those who had been scattered preached the word wherever they went" (Acts 8:1,4). And the church exploded with growth.

God took something evil – violent resistance to the people of God proclaiming the message of Jesus – and He redeemed it. The persecution became the fertile soil of Kingdom expansion. The church grew rapidly way beyond the borders of the City of David as the people who were scattered spread the message of Jesus. And it expanded beyond the Jewish people to the Samaritans and Gentiles. This persecution was one of the key factors in the rapid expansion of the church.

I really do believe that we are standing on the precipice of a historic kingdom moment but the church must be prepared in order to seize the opportunity that lies before us; we must embrace the purifying work of the Spirit in this season. There may be more openness to spiritual things in our society than ever before because of this. I have been talking to many pastors in this crisis who have indicated that their online attendance has been significantly higher than their Sunday morning attendance was before the crisis. People who were not previously attending church have started to tune in. I've talked to others who have already seen many people come to faith in Christ because of this present difficulty. This isn't like 9-11; that was an event, a tragic event that paused the world on its axis, but still a singular moment in time. This is a prolonged hardship that is impacting the entire world and will produce untold economic pain and expose undealt with emotional and spiritual issues. *When people's spiritual and emotional issues are surfaced, the Savior's healing power is magnified and compellingly attractive to those outside of faith.*

Historically, revival seldom occurs in times of blessing, prosperity, comfort and ease. Revival is most often birthed in times of war, famine, disease, and persecution. That is what makes this is an unprecedented opportunity to step into a historic kingdom moment. We must become the people we were born to be, so we can seize this historic kingdom opportunity. People often turn to God in times of hardship. If the church turns to God in this hardship and does the deep work of purification, and if we turn our hearts affections fully to Jesus in this season, we could be prepared to be the people that God needs to capture this kingdom moment in history.

The church in Acts 8 was a church empowered by the Holy Spirit, but they were huddled together in one place – Jerusalem. They needed to get out of Jerusalem and into the harvest field; they needed to carry the message to the world around them. They were prepared, but they needed to get into the presence of those who didn't believe all around the Roman Empire. Persecution pushed a prepared church out of the nest and into the harvest field.

Even then, God still needed to do some more preparation – He had to break them of prejudice. When the gospel started expanding to the Gentiles, the church had to deal with their resistance to Gentiles. Peter had a vision in Acts 10 showing him that God did not consider anyone unclean or unreachable. God led Cornelius to Peter and because of the vision that Peter had, Peter went and preached to Cornelius and his family. And while he was preaching to them the Holy Spirit fell upon them. But when the other believers heard Peter was preaching to the Gentiles, they questioned him. After hearing his story, they realized this was God at work and they yielded to the Spirit. The early believers had to be purged of their prejudice so that they could be released to fulfill their mission to bring the gospel to all peoples. We, too, need purging and mobilization into the harvest field. And it is often crisis that God uses to accomplish His redemptive purposes in the church so He can fulfill His redemptive mission in the world.

Impacting Community

It seems to me that many revivals remain localized. They impact a church or the church in a region, but they don't end up impacting the entire community; they don't change society. The church gets holy; the people of God turn away from sin and back to Jesus as their first love. There is unity in the body and there is life change. They are emptied of worldly affections and filled with the Spirit and passion for Jesus. That is a beautiful thing. But that's not enough. Jesus wants that purified, filled and empowered church to be on mission. Jesus wishes that none should perish, but that all should come to repentance and faith (2 Peter 3:9). Peter says that this is why Jesus delays his coming – because He doesn't want anyone to miss out on relationship with Him and their eternal home in heaven. Sometimes revivals have expanded beyond the doors of the church and have broken forth into a community as a spiritual awakening. The community turns to Jesus; souls are saved, lives are changed, society is impacted, social reform takes place. The world is marked by the movement of God. It starts with the church, but something in the environment opened the hearts of those outside of faith to be spiritually receptive. This is what happened in Acts – the church was purified and filled and mobilized on mission in power and the Roman Empire was impacted.

In my generation the church focused on evangelism, and missed God's call to fight for justice. In this generation the pendulum has swung toward justice, but we may be in danger of missing God's call to the mission of spreading the message of Jesus to those outside the church. God deeply cares for the oppressed. He wants us to fight for freedom and equality for those oppressed by gender bias and racial prejudice. I am grateful for the emphasis that this has received in these later years in the church. But I hear less and less of Jesus' heart for those who are spiritually lost and eternally separated from God apart from faith in Jesus. This stands as a divine opportunity to correct that. If the church is purged and mission is re-set in the hearts of the people of God, we could see a great harvest in this season. The things that matter to God need to matter to us and Jesus wishes that none should perish.

I think we stand on the brink of a unique and widespread opportunity for the message of Jesus to expand, perhaps for the first time in my life. I had a conversation with a young minister the other day. He said to me, "You have always been passionate, but listening to you in this season, there is something different. It feels like there is more passion, more urgency. Why?" The answer is because we are at a unique place in history. I have fought for revival my whole life. When I was 24 years old, the Lord laid out my life calling. He said, "You will plant a church; you will teach at seminary; you will write books and you will speak to leaders internationally. Everything you do, do for revival." That's my calling. The Lord has called me to fight for revival. I have prayed, preached, led, mentored and written for this one cause: revival. In my lifetime I have seen the Spirit working to prepare the church for renewal. I have seen life change. I have seen the Spirit come with power. I have seen people healed, delivered and filled with the Holy Spirit. I have seen an increasing number of leaders get on board with the things of the Spirit. I have seen God stirring a spiritual hunger within His people around the world, across a broad range of denominations. It has felt like the water level of the Spirit has been rising slowly over the past two decades within the church.

But this is different. This is a unique moment in history where the people outside of the church across the world are experiencing fear of the pandemic, fear of sickness, fear of death and fear of an increasing economic threat coming in the wake of this pandemic that is unparalleled in my years in ministry. Never before, in my lifetime, has the world been locked away in isolation. Never before has there been a widespread shutting down of all non-essential businesses. This is an unprecedented opportunity because this is an unparalleled happening. If the church goes all in for Jesus, does the deep work of the inner life, and allows God to redeem this crisis for their spiritual benefit, they will be ready for a potential spiritual openness like we have not seen.

Death makes people open to faith. I have led many people to Christ on their deathbed, people like Bud. They realize the end is coming and they want to know that they are ready to meet God. As a minister, I have often had intriguing conversations with people at funerals. Death opens people's minds to spiritual things. It is one thing when an old person dies, but it is an entirely different category of openness when a young person dies unexpectedly. Old people die – that's what happens to everyone in life, so that isn't as jarring or as eye-opening. But when death comes calling and beckons someone to an early and unexpected grave, people are shaken, and they are more responsive to spiritual conversation. It is always the funerals of the young that I have had the largest and most receptive crowds. The past few weeks in New York

City, I personally know two people who have died who are younger than me and had no pre-existing medical conditions. This is the kind of thing that shakes people.

Pain, also, makes people open to God. Whether it is physical pain, emotional pain, family pain, or financial pain, pain makes us grapple with the meaning of life. When you had hope in one thing, and that thing comes crashing down, you look for a new source of hope. *Sustained pain makes us scramble for rays of light in the darkness, sources of hope in the despair*. It makes us look for comfort that even lasts beyond the temporary solutions an impermanent world can offer. Pain makes us open to receive help, comfort, and love. When Christians love like Jesus, act like Jesus, serve like Jesus and give like Jesus, the world is drawn to Jesus and they are open to the Good News about Jesus, especially a world in great need.

Let us become the people we need to be. Let us empty ourselves of the worldly attachments, sin and dysfunction that is revealed through this crisis. Let us turn to Jesus wholeheartedly and be filled afresh with His Spirit. And then, purified, free and full, let us turn to the world in this great hour of need and act like Jesus would act. Let us seize this moment in redemptive history.

Chapter 5: For such a time as this

Esther is an interesting book in the Bible. It is the only book in the Bible that does not mention God's name. It is ten chapters long and yet God is never mentioned. You have to understand when you read the Bible that the Bible is all about God. It is a book about God and His ways and doings. God is the central figure, the hero in every story. It is never really a story about David or Nehemiah or Esther or the apostle Paul. It is a story about God and His dealings with people and His redemptive work with humanity. Given this, why then is there a book in the Bible that is ten chapters long yet never mentions God at all? It is not an accident; the author of the book is clearly trying to make a point to his audience and to us. The book was written at a time in redemptive history when the people of God felt like God had forgotten them and their plight and they felt like God was nowhere to be found. They were in a time of captivity and it felt like God had abandoned His people. But the author wanted them and us to understand that though there are times in life when it may seem like God is absent, His name may not be mentioned because He doesn't appear to be a main character on the stage of human happenings, yet God is directing the scenes of history toward His ultimate redemptive purposes.

Have you ever done one of those magic eye things? You stare at this page that just looks like a bunch of random dots and lines, and as you let your eyes relax, all of a sudden, a picture emerges. You now see the photo that is beneath the surface.

Esther is like that. We stare at the pages that never mention God and an invisible hand begins to emerge from the picture on the pages. It is the invisible hand of God that guides the events of human history. And it was the invisible hand of God that was guiding Esther and her people. Though the circumstances made it appear as though God were absent, the author leaves His name out of the book, the providential arrangement of the details made it apparent that God was very present indeed. The invisible hand of God is with us still today, even if the events of our day make it appear that He is absent.

Esther was chosen to be King Xerxes' wife. She was chosen in a beauty contest because Xerxes was angry with his first wife, Vashti, so he banished her. Esther was a Jew, but no one in authority knew that, not even Xerxes. An evil man named Haman rose to power in the King's court and he had a personal vendetta with the Jewish people. He had a particular animosity with a man named Mordecai, who would not bow down to him. This infuriated the self-absorbed Haman, but he wasn't satisfied with merely seeking vengeance against Mordecai for this slight. He plotted to kill all of the Jewish people, but Mordecai, who also just happened to be Esther's relative who raised her, came to Esther to save the Jewish people. It is in the happenstance of the details that we start to see the invisible hand of God emerge.

Esther was a young woman and she was naturally afraid of her circumstances. In that day and age, she was not allowed to approach the king without the king's explicit invitation. He had already banished one queen, and it wasn't beneath him to find a replacement for her too. Mordecai could see that she was fearful at the prospect of approaching the king to save her people, so he sent her a message. "Do not think that because you are in the king's house you alone of all the Jews will escape. For if you remain silent at this time, relief and deliverance for the Jews will arise from another place, but you and your father's family will perish. And who knows but that you have come to royal position for such a time as this?" (Esther 4:13-14). Mordecai felt certain that the invisible hand of God had positioned Esther to be the queen of the land at this unique time in history because this was God's plan for saving the Jewish people from destruction.

It may very well be that God has positioned you in history for such a time as this. This is a time like no other in my lifetime, providing us with an unmatched opportunity to advance the Kingdom. *These opportune times in Kingdom history are seldom available, but decidedly vital. These opportune times in Kingdom history are seldom convenient, but definitely crucial.* These are moments in Kingdom history when the world apparently pauses on its axil and Christians can stand in the gap and bring understanding, hope and healing to a world lost in chaos, fear and uncertainty. These opportune times in the Kingdom require prepared and willing servants to step into the gap, even at great risk, like Esther. We will be called upon to display courage that we didn't know we had. We will be called upon to draw from resources that are beyond our human strength. We will be called upon to display love that surpasses our natural limitations.

Seizing this Kingdom Moment

You have been born into a unique time in human history. You have been called and set apart by Jesus for such a time as this. Jesus didn't choose to put you in this moment in history by accident. He didn't make a mistake calling you into this opportune Kingdom moment. He didn't place you in this historic moment so you would wither in fright and shrink back into oblivion. He positioned you to be a light in the darkness, a conduit of His presence. And when God calls us to stand in the gap at a crucial moment in history, He supplies us with the strength, power and resources to rise up to the occasion.

Light is at its very best when darkness is at its very worst. It is indeed a dark hour in history, and it feels like the hour may get even darker as the economic storm clouds continue to form. But we are not the first generation to live in a dark hour. This can be one of those difference-making moments when, no doubt, the light is most needed and most evident in all of its beauty. Jesus said, "I am the light of the world" (John 8:12). He said to his followers, "You are the light of the world" (Matthew 5:14). The world never has a keener awareness of its need for light like it does when darkness reigns.

So, what can we do to seize this moment in Kingdom history? We talked last chapter about being the people we need to be. We have to do the work of the soul; we need to give the Lord access to our inner life so He can repair the damaged places in our souls. We have to consecrate ourselves fully to God in this hour and seek His face. We need to become the people that we were created and redeemed by God to be in order to seize the hour. That's where it begins. But after that, what steps can we take to partner with God in this crucial hour?

Pray for Revival

First, pray for revival in the church and for a great awakening in our world. Pray that God would redeem this hour in our lives to make us the purified and empowered citizens of heaven that are needed for such a time as this. Pray that God would turn these dark hours in history into illuminating moments for countless souls throughout the world.

We have lived through the most dramatic world view shift the world has ever known. Previously, when a world view shifted, it took a long time. Some new thoughts arose from some intellectual capital someplace on the planet, but it had to make its way over horseback across the land, and over the ocean to other continents In all, it took hundreds of years to change a world view. Not now. With the advent of the internet and social media, we are witnessing world views changing with alarming brevity. We have felt uncertain and unstable like we were standing in quicksand in these times of discontinuous change. But the world shifted from a modern world view to a postmodern world view in the past couple of decades. And the change has been dramatic.

The new world is more open to spiritual things than it previously has been though it is less open to traditional Christianity. In fact, what the new world has rejected was the old religious version of Christianity. But if Christians get renewed in this season, the new world will be open to Christians that live out their faith in vital ways. *Religion is repulsive, but Jesus has always been, is now and always will be, the most compelling person in human history.* When Jesus is portrayed and presented by imperfect but passionate followers of Christ, many people are irresistibly drawn to Him. Pray that we become those kinds of people and the world becomes open to Jesus in these times of crisis like never before. And pray that the people around us who don't know Jesus will be drawn by the Holy Spirit to Jesus like never before in our lifetimes. May a revival fire breakout in the church that leads to a spiritual awakening in our world.

Love

Second, if we are going to partner with God and seize this crucial moment in history, love is and always has been the key. We need to look like Jesus, love like Jesus and act like Jesus in these crucial times. We need to represent Him really well. Jesus said, "As the Father has loved me, so have I loved you. Now remain in my love" (John 15:9). In this season, we have to experience the perfect love of Jesus that drives out fear. Fear makes us selfish; selfishness makes us smell like the world. *Selfish acts can never draw people to a self-less Savior. But action marked with sacrificial selfless love will always attract people to Jesus.* Perfect love makes us act in Jesus-like ways that compels people to seek Him. The authentic love of Christ is irresistibly attractive to sinners of all generations. They may not choose to follow, but when people encounter the authentic love of Christ they are drawn to Jesus. When Jesus told his followers that they were the light of the world He said, "Let your light shine before others, that they may see your good deeds and glorify your Father in heaven" (Matthew 5:16). When Christians take up the selfless love of Jesus, non-believers are inspired to look to the Father.

Jesus went on to say, "My command is this: Love each other as I have loved you. Greater love has no one than this: to lay down one's life for one's friends" (John 15:12-13). I think the unity of Christians has always been and will always be critical to our mission to reach people with the Good News of the Gospel of the Kingdom. Jesus prayed for us in John 17. He said, "My prayer is not for them [the apostles] alone. I pray also for those who will believe in me through their message, that all of them may be one, Father, just as you are in me and I am in you. May they also be in us so that the world may believe that you have sent me." *Our unity is critical to the effectiveness of the mission of the church.* Yet, the church has often struggled with unity. *We argue over minor doctrinal differences and demonize people who have differing theological perspectives. We get trapped in theological minutia and tripped up on our mission.* All the while, we miss out on the essential unity of our mutual trust in Jesus Christ. It's killing the effectiveness of the church; it's repulsive to the lost and leaves them rejecting Christ because his children can't figure out how to get along.

My brother and I used to fight like two alley cats when we were kids. Once we had a friend come over to visit during a school vacation; he was supposed to stay with us for the entire week of our school break. But the kid stayed for about two days before calling his mother to come and take him home. He couldn't stand being in the dissention any longer. So, it is with the church today. Our fighting has caused people to reject the house of God and has hindered our mission. The people we are trying to attract to Jesus are repelled from the church because of our attacks on each other. But times of crisis often allow the church to put aside truly non-essential doctrinal differences and unite around Jesus and his mission. It is a critical hour for the family of God to start loving each other like healthy brothers and sisters in the family of God, so the world will be drawn to the family and not repulsed by it.

It is also vital that we love people outside the church like Jesus does, if we are going to reach them. Jesus was the only pure One who ever lived;

He lived without sin. Yet, sinners were never repelled by Him but irresistibly attracted to Him. They didn't feel judged by Him but accepted by Him. Why? Because He loved them. John 3:16f, "For God so loved the world that he gave his one and only Son, that whoever believes in him shall not perish but have eternal life. For God did not send his Son into the world to condemn the world, but to save the world through him." *Jesus came to save, not condemn. He came to redeem, not repel. He came to attract, not attack.* He came because we were lost and irreparably damaged by sin; we were separated from God and irretrievably removed from His presence without grace. He came to us because we couldn't go to Him. He came because He loved, and He welcomed sinners with open arms. He was the personification of holiness and yet prostitutes and the worst of sinners felt drawn to His loving presence. This is still the way to win people with the irrepressible love of Jesus that beckons lost and wandering souls back to God. Jesus doesn't judge those in sin, He loves those in sin so that they won't be judged. The church needs to be mobilized on a mission of love, just like Jesus.

Offer Practical Help

Third, if we are going to seize this critical kingdom moment, we need to turn our love into practical help. James said, "What good is it, my brothers and sisters, if people claim to have faith but have no deeds? Can such faith save them? Suppose a brother or sister is without clothes and daily food.

If one of you says to them, 'Go in peace; keep warm and well fed,' but does nothing about their physical needs, what good is it? In the same way, faith by itself, if it is not accompanied by action, is dead" (James 2:14-17). Faith without deeds is dead. *In this generation the proclamation of the gospel of the Kingdom without Christlike action has been readily dismissed as irrelevant by the masses who do not know Jesus.* This is going to be even more true in this current season. There is going to be real need and we will have an opportunity to demonstrate Jesus' authentic love in tangible ways. Words without actions will not win people. Jesus didn't just tell people God loved them; Jesus healed their diseases and cared for their broken hearts. He didn't just tell people they could be forgiven; He drove out their demons and set them free.

We are going to have to be marked by the generous love of God. That true love has to permeate our hearts so deeply we become free from the fear that causes people to selfishly hoard, because we trust God to provide enough for us that we allow Him to give generously through us. Selfless acts of generosity in this season of need will draw people to the Source of authentic love. As we detach from the things of this world and attach more radically to our heavenly citizenship, sacrificial generosity will once again set apart Christ followers from those around us.

In Acts, Luke reports, "All the believers were together and had everything in common. They sold property and possessions to give to anyone who had need. . . And the Lord added to their number daily those who were being saved" (Acts 2:45,47). *The unity and generosity of the believers made their message believable and their mission unstoppable.* In Acts 4, Luke says, "All the believers were one in heart and mind. No one claimed that any of their possessions was their own, but they shared everything they had. With great power the apostles continued to testify to the resurrection of the Lord Jesus. And God's grace was so powerfully at work in them that there were no needy persons among them. From time to time, those who owned land or houses sold them, brought the money from the sales and put it at the apostles' feet, and it was distributed to anyone who had need" (Acts 4:32-35). This is a remarkable story. No wonder the church was exploding with growth and transforming society. They didn't just proclaim the message of Jesus; they demonstrated the unity of the Spirit and the transformative love of Jesus through generous community. Who wouldn't be attracted to that? *Love without deeds is a message without power. Preaching without unity is a mission without impact. Mission without generosity is a church without appeal.*

But did you see the key to it all? "God's grace was so powerfully at work in them that there were no needy persons among them" (Acts 4:33-34). Grace can't just be a word that we believe. Grace can't just be a message that we proclaim. Grace can't just be a name on the church building that we attend. Grace has to be a powerful transformational reality in our inner being that changes our hearts and our lives. We must be so marked by the favor of God, so moved by the love of Christ that we are secured not by earth's comforts but by heaven's certainty. Grace must make its way out of our brains and into our lives so that our possessions can make their way out of our hearts and into our neighbor's hands. We must allow the Spirit of God access to the deep inner places of our souls so that we will be marked by the powerful work of grace that sets us free from the grip of this world. *When grace marks us with radical generosity, people around us will be moved to believe the love that drove Jesus to the cross.*

In Matthew 9:35-38, Jesus is moved with compassion because the crowds are harassed and helpless like sheep without a shepherd. Then he turns to the disciples and says, "The harvest is plentiful, but the workers are few. Ask the Lord of the harvest, therefore, to send out workers into his harvest field." The very next scene he sends them out – they become the answer to the prayer He invited them to pray. I believe this is likely going to be a time of harvest and we need to become the answer to our prayers for the harvest to be reaped. We, like the disciples, are going to have to roll up our sleeves and get involved. We are going to have to step out in obedient faith and demonstrate love in practical ways so that people are drawn to Jesus. They went out and spread the message of the Kingdom and prayed for the sick to be healed and the demonized to be delivered and people came to know the King.

Serve our Communities

Fourth, if we are going to seize this moment in kingdom history, our practical love is going to require us to serve our communities. Meeting real needs with practical service is winsome. The mother of James and John once came to Jesus and asked if her two boys could get the primary seats in the Kingdom – on Jesus' left and right. The other disciples heard about this and they were ticked. They were always jockeying for position and they didn't like this underhanded move! Jesus called them all together and said, "You know that the rulers of the Gentiles lord it over them, and their high officials exercise authority over them. Not so with you. Instead, whoever wants to become great among you must be your servant, and whoever wants to be first must be your slave – just as the Son of Man did not come to be served, but to serve, and to give his life as a ransom for many" (Matthew 20:25-28). *Service is the mindset of the King and must be reflected in the heart of his servants.*

Sometimes churches have taken up a strategy of serving their communities. They have given away free car washes, handed out water in parks, and done other random acts of kindness. I think these have some impact on the positive attitude of a community toward a church. But they are low impact evangelistic tools. However, when we serve someone in a desperate situation and we meet their real need with genuine compassion, that marks their life and moves their heart toward Jesus. When we bring food to people who don't have enough to eat, that opens their hearts. When we gather together as believers to fix a neighbor's bathroom that is in disrepair, that changes their outlook on Jesus.

We will have to learn how to ask good questions and become good listeners in this season, so that we can discern the real needs that are in our midst and then act to meet them. We cannot simply try to act on what we perceive as needs. Every region will have unique needs coming out of this crisis and we are going to have to become good listeners and learn how to nuance our acts of service to fit the felt needs of our specific community. Churches that mobilize their people on mission to meet real needs with the love of Christ are going to be a beacon of light in a dark night. *The more effective we become at addressing felt needs, the more impactful we will be in advancing the Gospel.* Church leaders are going to have to mobilize people on mission and coordinate service efforts to solve real problems.

Often Churches are reluctant to join other organizations in our community as they attempt to address the needs around us. Rather than joining a local organization that feeds the homeless, they start their own homeless ministry. But this is no time to do everything on our own. This is a time to form partnerships, to come alongside others, to help coordinate efforts, and to join the cause in meeting needs. We can love the people we serve shoulder to shoulder with, and we can love the people we are serving and demonstrate to all that Jesus sees, and Jesus cares. When social isolation lifts, service opportunities will rise.

In the New Testament, there is no such thing as an authentic proclamation of the gospel without a demonstration of power. Jesus proclaims the Gospel of the Kingdom and then He heals the sick and casts out demons. If we proclaim that Jesus has victory over sin, then we must demonstrate that victory by showing how He overcomes the effects of sin. We need to serve people under the power of the Holy Spirit. We need to demonstrate the power and presence of God is imminent and transformational. When acts of service are done with a heart of love and marked by the presence and power of God, they are unmistakably compelling.

In Matthew 10 when Jesus sent out the disciples, He told them: "As you go, proclaim this message: 'The kingdom of heaven has come near.' Heal the sick, raise the dead, cleanse those who have leprosy, drive out demons. Freely you have received, freely give" (Matthew 10:7-8). The disciples show up in people's neighborhoods and interact with people who have real needs. They proclaimed that God's kingdom was near and available. Heaven was invading earth and overturning sin and all of its effects. Jesus, the King, had come to reverse the effects of the fall, to restore things to the way they were intended to be. Then, the disciples laid hands on people in Jesus' name and the sick were healed. They commanded demons to leave those who had been tormented and tortured souls were set free. In the regions of the world where the gospel is rapidly expanding, this is still part of the regular strategy and experience of the church. They preach the gospel and demonstrate it with power – just like the early church. They don't just say that Jesus overcame sin; they demonstrate that Jesus overcame sin by demolishing sin's strongholds with the power of the risen Christ.

Our service needs to be marked by Jesus' love and power so that destitute people in despairing situations can see the hope of heaven in the midst of their hellish circumstances. We need to seek His face and pray for His power to be manifest in our midst for the sake of those for whom Jesus has died. But if we give Him our uncompromised affection and seek His face with unadulterated loyalty, our lives will be more saturated with His presence and power. It will require us to risk more than we have. Our next level with God always lies beyond the boundaries of our current experience and the only way to get there is to risk more than we are comfortable with. We have to step out of our comfort zones and step into faith-filled risks if we are going to see the power of God.

A number of years ago I went to Brazil on a mission trip. One village that we went to was desperately destitute. We held a healing evangelism service and the people came. They came because they had no alternatives. To get to the nearest hospital they had to take a 24-hour boat ride, and then they had to pay for everything out of their own pocket – every needed medical supply. They had no money to do this and they had no recourse. So, when we did a healing evangelism service they came, lining up for prayer. I'm not sure I've ever seen more desperate people clinging to the hope of a heavenly intervention. One lady I prayed for had a tumor and, apart from a miracle, she had no hope. I have never seen anyone else come for prayer with such longing in her eyes. Her desperation was the birthing ground for faith and when I prayed in Jesus' name, her tumor disappeared.

This season could birth new desperation in the hearts of people, new faith in the souls of God's children and new service opportunities in our communities that result in a harvest of freshly redeemed lives. Let's be ready to step in and serve wherever Jesus calls us. Let's be eager to step out in risky faith and pray for those in need around us. Let's step in with a helping hand, a loving word, a practical act of service, a faith filled prayer or whatever else God calls us to. Let's anticipate what God can do in releasing his power to reap a harvest.

The Hope of Heaven

Fifth, if we are going to capture this kingdom opportunity, we will need to proclaim the hope of heaven. As a means to engage people in an evangelistic conversation people used to ask, "If you died tonight would you go to heaven?" It worked more often back in its day, but over time people became less concerned with the afterlife and the effectiveness of that strategy ran its course. I am not suggesting we bring that approach back, but I am saying that with so many people dying in our world and so many of our communities being touched by death because of COVID-19 and with so many people fearful, people need hope. They need the hope of heaven.

As I said earlier, death does tend to make people more open to talk about spiritual things and eternity. This is particularly true when someone dies tragically, or a young person dies unexpectedly. This week I heard a story about a young medical worker that caught the virus and died. I read an article this week about an infant dying from COVID-19. A young doctor in New York City committed suicide after being overwhelmed with caring for so many dying patients; she had no history of depression. I talked to a parent whose child had the virus yesterday and they wept as I prayed with them. These are scary times and many people are terrified – terrified of getting sick, terrified of dying, terrified of losing people that they love. People are edgy, sometimes even hostile to others who get too close, because of the real fear that is in their hearts. I have already had multiple conversations with people who are afraid to die just like my friend Bud was. They need comfort; they need the hope of heaven. I talked to a pastor last week who led someone to Christ because they called the church afraid to die and looking for hope.

Jesus talked to Martha after her brother died and he said, "I am the resurrection and the life. Anyone who believes in me will live, even though they die; and whoever lives by believing in me will never die" (John 11:25). Jesus promised us life abundant and life eternal. Jesus then conquered death, left behind the grave clothes and the empty tomb, and paved the way for us to live forever with Him in heaven. This is why Paul said for him to live is Christ, and to die is gain. We have this eternal hope that we can share. Our calm in this crisis can be as real as our confidence in our eternal home in heaven. And we can be a voice of peace in the pain, a voice of hope in the helplessness.

I was thinking about this obscure passage in Matthew 27 this week: "And when Jesus had cried out again in a loud voice, he gave up his spirit. At that moment the curtain of the temple was torn in two from top to bottom. The earth shook, the rocks split and the tombs broke open. The bodies of many holy people who had died were raised to life. They came out of the tombs after Jesus' resurrection and went into the holy city and appeared to many people" (Matthew 27:51-53). Jesus' death was so powerful, it broke the power of death over the saints who had been before him. *The death of Christ unshackled the chains of death that held these saints captive and they walked out of the tombs. I wonder if this was the moment that Satan knew he was defeated.* Before this he must have had some hope that his plan to kill Jesus would ensure his victory and humanity's ultimate and final defeat. But when Jesus yelled, "It is finished" and the temple veil was torn from top to bottom, a veil too high for humans to reach, access was opened to the Holy of Holies; access was opened to the presence of God. This bizarre rending of the veil must have rattled Satan. But the sealing moment was when the present death of Christ overcame death's grip on the godly people of the past. *How could a death be so powerful it produced life?* How could the end of one life release new life to dead people? This was the moment in time when the sin and all of its effects were dealt a final blow and eternal life started bursting into the souls of the once living and now alive again. Only Jesus. This is the hope of the world. This is what people need to know in this frightening hour where death appears to reign. There is life in Christ. Jesus defeated death with his death, and He offers life eternal to all who believe.

Always be sure to factor in eternity. The protection of God is eternally secure even if it is temporarily interrupted by death. Death is a temporary reality that has been permanently defeated. I always think we have to factor in eternity to fully understand the promises of God and to secure our hope. Many people need the hope of heaven in the face of death. They need to know that Jesus defeated death and they can have eternal life.

Hope

Sixth, if we are going to maximize this moment in kingdom history, we have to become soul-savvy people who can offer hope to the spiritually and emotionally suffering. Crisis really does have a way of revealing the cracks in our interior lives. It is one of the reasons why we are more open to change during times of hardship, because we feel these cracks in our soul and we are open to help. I have often said that I believe *Soul Care* will be a gateway to evangelism in this generation. I think more people will come to faith in Christ because they know they are broken in need of Healer than because they know they are sinners in need of a Savior. That is a missiological statement, not a theological statement. I am not saying they aren't sinners in need of a Savior. They are sinners just like us, and they need the Savior. I am saying that most often what will draw them to Christ is their awareness of their interior pain and heartache and dysfunction. Their brokenness is so compelling, they are desperate for hopeful answers and real solutions to their problems. In a season like this, they are going to feel the foundation crumbling and the walls cracking more than ever and they are going to be open to authentic solutions. Jesus is the Healer, and no one does life change like Jesus.

I have noticed in the past year that often as I travel the world and do Soul Care Conferences, I meet someone at the conference who is not a Christ follower. They came because they knew something was 'off' in their inner world; they had some presenting problem that they couldn't overcome. They had an addiction or an emotional pain or a heartache that they couldn't heal. They came, knowing full well that it was a Jesus-centered conference. Though they were not followers of Jesus, they came because they heard it offered help to the soul-weary traveler. Multiple times now in Soul Care Conferences in these past few months someone has come to faith in Christ.

In a postmodern world, we are more aware of our brokenness than we are of our sinfulness. And brokenness can make people open to Jesus, because Jesus is the Healer. This current crisis is only going to exasperate that inner brokenness that we feel and open doors in people's hearts to the Gospel of the Kingdom and to Jesus the King. This crisis lies before us as an opportunity like no other in my lifetime. Anxiety has already become the number one mental health problem in North America – this crisis will only increase the number of people wrestling with anxiety. More people will slide into depression. More people will struggle with anger and domestic violence will increase – in New York there has already been an increase. More people will have relational conflict and pain in their homes as they are forced together in stressful times. Painful emotional realities are often the gateway to redemptive spiritual possibilities.

We cannot, however, give what we do not possess. When Jesus sent his disciples to heal the sick, cast out demons, and preach the Kingdom, He said to them, "Freely you have received, freely give." We can't give what we don't have. We only have authority over that which we walk in victory. If we are going to offer people freedom, we must be free. If we are going to proclaim peace in the storm, we must carry the peace of Christ in our center. If we are going to offer people wholeness, we must give Jesus access to our inner being so that He can make us whole. We must take the journey with Him, so we can go on the journey with them.

The End?

There is a myriad of responses to this current crisis. Some people are dismissive and say this is no worse than the flu and the world response is ridiculous. I am not in that camp. I've talked to friends who are medical doctors in New York City and who have a very different opinion. I've known some of these people for a long time; they are reasonable people who do not have a history of over reacting. They have described it to me like a war zone in NYC. One of my doctor friends said that she has never seen anything like it and talked about the post-traumatic stress that would affect medical people when this was over.

There are others who think that the virus is serious, but that our world-wide response is going to have worse ramifications than the disease itself. I actually agree with this to a point. I have no doubt that if we just let the virus run its course under our normal living conditions it would kill hundreds of thousands of people. I do think that we need to take precautions. I think we should practice social distancing; I think that those who are most vulnerable to the disease should stay home as much as humanly possible. My Dad, for example, has acute myeloid leukemia. If he is exposed to COVID-19, he likely will not live. My Mom and Dad need to stay home and take every precaution. But I am not convinced that we should have everyone socially isolate and shut down all non-necessary businesses.

My problem is that I am not convinced that our approach is actually going to work. I referred to Mark Woolhouse in the introduction. He said that social distancing as a temporary strategy will not work. We either need vaccination or we need to have 60% of the population to develop immunities to the disease through exposure. Vaccination is likely more than a year away still and even if they develop a vaccine, it will take much longer than that to immunize everyone. Can we shut down the world's economy for another year or two without expecting to have cataclysmic results that impact far more people than the disease itself? With our current strategy of temporary social isolation, when we release people back into the work force, what will prevent the virus from spreading again? Several cities that had an outbreak early on, and now have released people to return to work, have had a fresh outbreak. I think Woolhouse is right. And I don't think we can use social isolation as a permanent strategy without permanently wrecking our world economy. I think in the end that will potentially cost us more lives than the virus itself because of poverty, suicides, increase in domestic violence and political upheaval that may even lead to revolutions. It wouldn't be the first time in history. I think we need a different plan than the one we currently have – a plan that takes the disease serious but doesn't put the entire world economy on hold. That's not the purpose of this book – it is simply an observation and my opinion.

Then there are those who think that this is the end of the world. I have talked to believers and unbelievers alike who have spoken of this current crisis in apocalyptic terms. Jesus said, "You will hear of wars and rumors of wars but see to it that you are not alarmed. Such things must happen, but the end is still to come. Nation will rise against nation, and kingdom against kingdom. There will be famines and earthquakes in various places. All these are the beginnings of birth pains" (Matthew 24:6-8). I think there is ample cause to believe that things will get difficult as the end approaches, but that doesn't mean this is the end. It isn't the first time in history that we have been through cataclysmic times and people thought it was the end of the world.

To be truthful, I don't know if we are coming to the end of time. Jesus said, "About the day or hour no one knows, not even the angels in heaven, nor the Son, but only the Father" (Matthew 24:36). People have been predicting end times stuff since the beginning and they have been nothing but wrong so far. We are clearly in the last days – the last days, biblically speaking, are from the time that Christ rose until the time that Christ returns. Paul saw himself in the last days, so did Peter. That was the way the New Testament writers wrote and spoke and lived. And I think that leads us to the greater point at hand.

The point that Jesus was making to us in his teaching about the end of the age is that we should be ready. We shouldn't be taken by surprise or caught off guard when the last day in history finally arrives. We should vigilantly live like the end is upon us. How would that change your life? How would it reset your priorities? How would it refocus your passion? The Apostle John wrote, "We know that when Christ appears, we shall be like him, for we shall see him as he is. All who have this hope in him purify themselves, just as he is pure" (1 John 3:2-3). The New Testament writers call us to live with urgency and wholehearted devotion because the end is imminent – it could be here at any time. And you don't want to be caught napping when the Master returns.

That's often the benefit that crises afford us – they prepare the heart and they cause us take God seriously. They shake our confidence in ourselves and in our plans and cause us to take stock of life. They demand that we re-evaluate our priorities and put God first and purify ourselves. In short, they cause us to prepare ourselves to live for heaven, just in case our end is near. That's why Jesus concluded this teaching on the end of the age with these words: "Therefore keep watch, because you do not know on what day your Lord will come. But understand this: If the owner of the house had known at what time of night the thief was coming, he would have kept watch and would not have let his house be broken into. So you also must be ready, because the Son of Man will come at an hour when you do not expect him" (Matthew 24:42-44). So, the big question is simply this: Are you ready? *Are you living your life in such a way that if Jesus came tomorrow morning you would be pleased with the account you would give to Him? Is Jesus your first love, your central priority, your highest loyalty? Does Jesus have your fullest attention, your deepest affection, your wholehearted surrender?* Have you given Him full access? Are you entirely consecrated to Him? Are you living with the vigilant, urgent, and passionate dedication that the last days call you into? Are you taking holiness seriously?

Jesus said, "Who then is the faithful and wise servant, whom the master has put in charge of the servants in his household to give them their food at the proper time? It will be good for that servant whose master finds him doing so when he returns. Truly I tell you, he will put him in charge of all his possessions. But suppose that servant is wicked and says to himself, 'My master is staying away a long time,' and he then begins to beat his fellow servants and to eat and drink with drunkards. The master of that servant will come on a day when he does not expect him and at an hour he is not aware of. He will cut him to pieces and assign him a place with the hypocrites, where there will be weeping and gnashing of teeth" (Matthew 24:45-51). I don't want that to be my story. If this is the final hour of history, then I want to be ready. If it is not the final hour, then I want to live like it is with total abandon for Jesus and His mission. I want to give the lone Worthy One my wholehearted affections and my undying passion and my relentless consecrated service to His eternal cause. Do you think it is possible to get to heaven and regret that you gave Jesus your all?

After Jesus talks to them about being ready for the end of the age, He goes on to tell them three parables in a row about the Kingdom at the end of the age. The first parable is the parable of the ten virgins (Matthew 25:1-13). The ten virgins went out to meet the bridegroom. They all brought lamps, but only five of them were wise enough to bring extra oil. They simply weren't prepared. The bridegroom was slow in coming, or so it appeared, but at midnight the call went out that he had arrived. The foolish virgins had run out of oil and they appealed to the wise virgins to let them borrow some. But the wise virgins wouldn't share, lest they be left with none also and miss the bridegroom. The foolish virgins went out to buy some and missed the bridegroom and they missed the big wedding. Jesus concluded with these words, "Therefore keep watch, because you do not know the day or the hour" (Matthew 25:13). Keep watch over the oil of the Spirit in your soul. Keep watch over the first love of your life. Let your spiritual fire burn bright, and if it has dimmed some, then let this hour of crisis become a redeeming hour in your life. Go after God with all of your heart until your lamp is re-lit for Jesus, the oil of the Spirit is plentiful, the fire of God burns bright and you are ready for the hour before you. Whatever is preventing you from loving Jesus with all your heart address it, surrender it, and remove it in this season. Get ready.

The second parable Jesus tells is the parable of talents (Matthew 25:14-30). In this parable the master goes away on a long journey, but he calls in his servants and entrusts his wealth to them. He gives one guy five bags of gold, one guy two bags of gold and the last guy one bag of gold. He gave it to them according to their ability. He didn't give them more than they could handle, nor did he require more than they could produce. The first two guys invest what has been entrusted to them and they double it. They both receive the same commendation from the master when he returns, "Well done, good and faithful servant! You have been faithful with a few things; I will put you in charge of many things. Come and share your master's happiness." But the last guy buried his bag of gold. He said to the master, "I knew that you were a hard man, harvesting where you have not sown and gathering where you have not scattered seed. So I was afraid and went out and hid your gold in the ground. See, here is what belongs to you." But why does he think the master is a hard man? There is absolutely no indication of this in the story. The answer likely has to do with the fact that the master gave him less than the other two. He was envious. Envy begins with the question, "What about me?" And ends with the accusation that God isn't fair. Envy is always an accusation against the goodness of God. It causes us to withdraw our hearts from full engagement because we compare ourselves with others and feel as though we have been given the short end of the stick. In the end, the master took his bag of gold and gave it to the guy who now had ten.

The lesson for us is to be wholeheartedly involved in the service of the Master for all our days. Part of being ready means we are faithful servants who are deeply involved in the Master's business, the Master's mission. That means we will have to deal with the soul issues that prevent us from full engagement – in this man's case, it was envy. *We have to empty the suitcase of our souls from our resentments, our petty jealousies and our passion robbing heart issues.* Everything that we have in life is a gift from the Master and we are managers, stewards of the Master's wealth. One day we will all given an account for what we did with that which the Master entrusted to us for His business. It is God's money, God's talents, God's gifts that He has graciously given to us to manage for the advance of His Kingdom. This is why it is foolish for us to trust our wealth and to draw comfort from our belongings, rather than from the Master who is the source of all things. He will only judge you according to what you have been given. What are you doing with what you have been given? Have you detached your possessions from your heart so you can fully attach your affections to the King and His Kingdom? Have you dedicated your time, your treasures, your talents, and your tears (your passions) to Jesus for His Kingdom purposes? Are you all in, sold out, wholly and holy His?

The last parable is the parable of the sheep and the goats (Matthew 25:31-46). This is a parable about the final judgment at the end of time. "When the Son of Man comes in his glory, and all the angels with him, he will sit on his glorious throne. All the nations will be gathered before him, and he will separate the people one from another as a shepherd separates the sheep from the goats" (Matthew 25:31-32). To the good ones, the sheep in the parable, he will say, "Come, you who are blessed by my Father; take your inheritance, the kingdom prepared for you since the creation of the world. For I was hungry and you gave me something to eat. I was thirsty and you gave me something to drink, I was a stranger and you invited me in. I needed clothes and you clothed me, I was sick and you looked after me, I was in prison and you came to visit me" (Matthew 25:34-36). But the people are confused because they didn't actually do any of these things for Jesus, so Jesus has to explain to them, "Truly I tell you, whatever you did for one of the least of these brothers and sisters of mine, you did for me" (Matthew 25:40). The other group that is separated out is remonstrated for the very things that this group is commended for – they didn't feed Him, clothe Him, invite Him, care for Him, visit Him. What they withheld from the least of these, they withheld from Him.

The Kingdom of God is the reversal of everything that went wrong with the world when sin entered the world. It is the restoration of the way things were supposed to be. So, we cannot be followers of the King unless we are involved His restoring work. Jesus was involved in healing the sick, casting out demons, caring for the poor, helping the disenfranchised and forgotten, and administering justice to the oppressed. This is the work of the King; it is the business of the Kingdom. Are you wholeheartedly engaged in the business of the King? Are you doing the work of the Kingdom? Once again, Jesus' point is: Are you ready?

If this is the end of time, and Jesus returns tomorrow, are you ready? I don't mean have you prayed a sinner's prayer and if you died tonight would you go to heaven. That's a good place to start, but that isn't the end game. That isn't at all what the parables are asking. Is the oil of the Spirit plentiful in your soul? Are you living in the current fullness of the Holy Spirit? Is the fire of God burning bright in your heart? Is Jesus your first love? Does your love for Jesus translate into your wholehearted investment into the Kingdom of God? Are you hungry and actively pursuing the presence of God? Are you investing all that God has entrusted to you into the Master's business? Are you actively, passionately and vigilantly engaged in the work of the Kingdom? Are you doing the work of Jesus – giving to the poor, caring for the sick, helping the captives get free, attending to the least of these? The way you do it, and the way I do it may differ based on our gifts and calling, but all of us are to be fully engaged.

If you aren't ready to give an account, then now is the time to do business with God and get ready. Engage in the necessary work of the heart. Now is the time.

In 2006 I had the same dream three nights in a row. In the dream an old woman came to me and prophesied a coming revival. I was sitting in a sports bar and she conveyed to me my role in this coming move of the Spirit. My role involved speaking, writing, traveling around the world and working with church leaders. Then she said, "Pray for him." The scene became dark and I found myself in a battle with a large demonic spirit. This giant was attacking me with a big sword. I had a little sword, a dagger, and I was fending him off and quoting Scripture at him in this spiritual battle. It was the sword of the Spirit. Eventually, I was able to overcome, I thrust the sword through him, and he died. Then I was attacked by panthers, one by one, I killed them off until finally the battle was over. I made my way up a large staircase and back into the mall where the sports bar was located, and I saw a Latina woman who was cleaning. I knew she was a prophetess and I asked her, "What is the sign of the coming revival?" She said to me, "The New Orleans Saints are going to win the Super Bowl." That was in December of 2006. On February 7, 2010 the New Orleans Saints won the Super Bowl.

At the beginning of this year I started praying that this would be a year when the Spirit was poured out in a new and fresh way, because this was the tenth anniversary of the Saints victory. I prayed and fasted as I sensed an urgency in my spirit that God could do something new in 2020. And then came COVID-19. This is not the kind of answer to prayer that I was hoping for, but it is the kind of crisis that God can redeem. Let the redeeming work of God begin in me and you. Let us prepare ourselves. Let us get ready. Let us prepare ourselves to be the kind of people that God can use in this kind of time in history. It may very well be that we stand on the precipice of an unprecedented opportunity in Kingdom history. May we be the kind of people that God can use in such a time as this.

ALSO BY ROB REIMER

Soul Care: 7 Transformational Principles for a Healthy Soul

Brokenness grasps for the soul of humanity. We are broken body, soul, broken body, soul, and spirit, and we need the healing touch of Jesus. *Soul Care* explores seven principles that are profound healing tools of God: securing your identity, repentance, breaking family sin patterns, forgiving others healing wounds, overcoming fears, and deliverance.

Dr. Reimer challenges readers to engage in an interactive, roll-up-your-sleeves and get messy process—a journey of self-reflection, Holy Spirit inspiration, deep wrestling, and surrender. It is a process of discovering yourself in true community and discovering God as He pierces through the layers of your heart.

Life change is hard. But these principles, when packaged together and lived out, can lead to lasting transformation, freedom, and a healthy soul. *Soul Care* encourages you to gather a small group of comrades in arms, read and process together, open your souls to one another, access the presence and power of God together, and journey into the freedom and fullness of Christ.

Transformational Soul Care DVD Teaching Series

Rob's first video teaching series is an in-depth guide to Soul Care. Great for individuals, small groups, or church wide curriculum, this series will be an invaluable guide to anyone who is going after freedom and fullness in Christ, or endeavoring to lead others along that journey.

River Dwellers: Living in the Fullness of the Spirit

Have you ever wished there was more to your Christian life? Too often the Christian life is reduced to going to church, attending meetings, serving God, and doing devotions. But Jesus promised us abundant life- a deep, intimate, satisfying connection with the living God. How do we access the abundant life that Jesus promised? The key is the presence and life of the Holy Spirit within us.

Jesus said that the Spirit of God flows within us like a river; He is the River of Life. But we need to dwell in the river in order to access the Spirit's fullness.

In this book, Dr. Reimer offers a deep look at life in the Spirit and provides practical strategies for dwelling in the River of Life. Rob explores the fullness of the Spirit, tuning in to the promptings of the Spirit, walking in step with the Spirit, and developing sensitivity to the presence of the God in our lives. This resource will guide you toward becoming a fulltime river dweller, even during life's most difficult seasons, when the river seems to run low.

Pathways to the King: Living a Life of Fullness and Power

We need revival. The church in America desperately needs revival. There are pockets of it happening, but we need another Great Awakening. About forty years ago, the church was impacted by the church growth movement. The goal of the movement to get the church focused on the Great Commission- taking the Good News about Jesus to the entire world. The church was off mission, and the movement was a necessary course correction. But it didn't work. Many people came to Christ as a result of this outreach emphasis, and we can be grateful to that. More churches are now focused on evangelism, helping people come to know Jesus, than they were before the movement. But we have fewer people (by percentage) attending church now than ever before in the history of the United States. We need revival.

This book is about how we can usher in revival and about the price we must pay to experience it. Dr. Reimer believes we have a part to play in seeing the next great spiritual awakening. God wants us to be carriers of His kingdom. He wants us to experience the reality and fullness of His kingdom, and he wants us to expand the kingdom to others, just like Jesus did. To do that, we must follow eight Kingdom Pathways of Spiritual Renewal: Personalizing our Identity in Christ, Pursuing God, Purifying Ourselves, Praising, Praying Kingdom Prayers, Claiming Promises, Passing the Tests, and Persisting. These eight pathways are discussed in great detail, are securely rooted in biblical truths, and are illustrated by compelling examples from Scripture and from Dr. Reimer's life, the lives of believers in his community, and in the lives of great Christians throughout history.

Deep Faith : Developing Faith that Releases the Power of God

Jesus said, "Very truly I tell you, all who have faith in me will do the works that I have been doing, and they will do even greater things than these" (John 14:12). The extraordinary promise of Jesus is that we can do Kingdom works that He did - cast out demons, heal the sick, save the lost and set the captives free.

Jesus wants to advance his Kingdom through us. But this promise comes with a condition: the level of our Kingdom activity is dependent upon our faith.

There are promises in Heaven that God wants to release, but they cannot be released without faith.

There are miracles that God wants to do that cannot be done without faith. There are answers to prayer that God wants to unleash that cannot be unleashed without faith. There are works of the Kingdom that God wants to accomplish that cannot be accomplished unless the people of God develop deeper faith. But there is hope for all of us, because faith can be developed.

Faith opens doors and creates opportunities for accessing God's power against all odds. Faith is a difference maker, a future shaper, a bondage breaker, a Kingdom mover. In his latest book, Dr. Rob Reimer challenges readers to develop deep faith that can release the works of the Kingdom. Faith is not static; it is dynamic. We can and must take an intentional path toward developing our faith if we want to see the works of the Kingdom in greater measure.

Made in the USA
Middletown, DE
12 November 2024